how to survive as a govern
Catholic Sch

A guide for all governors including priests, parents, teachers, support staff and those responsible for governor training

CONTENTS

Foreword, by Archbishop Malcolm McMahon OP		Page 2
Introduction		Page 3
Chapter 1	*Guardians of the vision*	Page 4
Chapter 2	*Standing on firm foundations*	Page 24
Chapter 3	*The challenge of forming the right team for the mission*	Page 42
Chapter 4	*People of innovation, challenge and change*	Page 54
Chapter 5	*Review and self-evaluation: on message – on mission – on task*	Page 70
Chapter 6	*What is expected of governors when Ofsted calls?*	Page 94
Chapter 7	*The role of the priest on the governing body*	Page 112
Chapter 8	*Prayers and praying together as governors*	Page 128

FOREWORD

There are two and a half thousand Catholic schools in England and Wales, and this means that many more thousands of Catholics serve on their governing bodies. Sister Judith Russi, in producing this guide, has made the role of being a school governor accessible to those who have this responsibility or are considering it. I hope that it will encourage many more to offer their time and skills in this wonderful way to help our children and to serve the wider society.

Parents bear the prime responsibility for educating their children, but the Church does not expect them to do this alone. Our Catholic schools, of which we are rightly proud, help parents to fulfil the promise they make at their children's baptism, and help our children to root themselves into the wider family of God's Church. They should be places in which everyone is treated with utmost respect, regardless of their background or academic ability, and helped to grow and develop so that their God-given potential can be fully realised and expressed.

School governors and directors of academy trusts have an extremely important role to play in our schools, and there are various ways in which they do this. Formally, there are meetings of the governing body and its various committees, which ensure that the school is being true to its mission as a Catholic school, is maintaining as high as possible a standard of teaching and learning, and is being managed efficiently and effectively in accordance with the Church's teaching and the law of England and Wales.

But governors, whether they have been appointed by the bishop as foundation governors, elected by parents as parent governors, or represent the staff or local authority, have another, informal but nevertheless vital, role of supporting and challenging the head teacher, Senior Leadership Team, staff and pupils by being regular visitors to the school, by asking questions of all members of the school family, and by being a link between the school and the wider community.

This book will make an important contribution to the development of our schools; by helping governors to understand more fully their role, it will help them to help our schools to be lively, creative and welcoming communities after the example of Jesus Christ, who came into our world that we may "have life, and have it to the full" (John 10:10)

+ Malcolm McMahon OP

Most Reverend Malcolm McMahon OP
Archbishop of Liverpool
Chairman of the Catholic Education Service

INTRODUCTION

How to Survive as a Governor in a Catholic School is for everyone who is appointed to a Catholic school in a governance role. Throughout the book I will be using the term "governor" to include both the new category of board of directors for academies as well as those schools who are governed by governing bodies. A "governor" is anyone appointed or elected to a position on a board whose chief responsibility is fulfilling the mission of the Church in education.

So is this book just for Catholics?

No. This book has been written for everyone who is part of a board or governing body. While the majority of board members will be Catholic there are members who are appointed from the local authority and parents who may well be of other faiths or none. This book is to help all governors better understand the mission of the Catholic Church in education.

What about the independent sector?

There are 137 independent Catholic schools, all governed by governing bodies who have the same responsibility of ensuring that they too are fulfilling their role in the mission of the Church in education.

A tool for developing the governing body

Throughout the book we have built in some exercises and questions for you to discuss as a governing body. Each chapter has been designed to work as a means of development and training, focusing on one aspect of your role and mission at a time. Chapter 1 will focus on your role as governors, guardians of the teachings and traditions of the Church. Chapter 2 moves into governor responsibilities under Canon Law and what they mean for us today. Formation for governors is often in short supply, so in Chapter 3 we explore ways in which governors can find the necessary help. Chapter 4 will discuss some of the contemporary challenges and issues facing governors today. Chapter 5 offers governors some tools for carrying out an audit within the Catholic context. Many governors are concerned about Ofsted and what is expected of them; so hopefully you will find some useful pointers in Chapter 6. Chapter 7 takes a careful look at the role of the priest governor through the eyes of priests today. Finally, Chapter 8 offers you a wide range of prayer ideas and suggestions for your meetings, times of reflection and private prayers as a governor.

A resource for reflection

Governors are very busy people who have day jobs either at home or in the workplace. Time is always at a premium. Therefore we will be offering you opportunities to stop and reflect on a question, poem or short text to help you to deepen your understanding of your ministry at the close of each chapter.

CHAPTER 1

Guardians of the vision

Upon Jesus' arrival in heaven, a vast host of angels greeted him. After the formalities, they asked him whom he had left behind on earth to finish the work he had begun.

Jesus replied, "Just a small group of men and women who love me." "That's all?" asked the angels, astonished. "What if this tiny group should fail?" Jesus replied, "I have no other plans."

Author unknown

To be a guardian of a vision might well seem somewhat mythical, straight from the writings of the ancient Greeks. However, that is exactly what we have been mandated to do. The following true story gives us a glimpse into what this might mean today.

A short story

Twenty years ago I visited the reservation owned by the Seneca Nation – a people with a proud and rich history, the largest of six Native American nations in New York State, whose democratic government pre-dates that of the United States Constitution.

The visit was challenging, to say the least, not to mention heartbreaking. However, what I was to experience on my last day with these amazing people was something that has left a deep and lasting impression on me. I asked if it might be possible for me to meet the Chief.

"Yes, of course," came the immediate reply.

I was driven for some twenty minutes, way out into the roughest and most remote part of the reservation. Eagerly I looked for what I thought would be the home of the Chief. Surely it would stand out from the rest of the poor dwellings, larger, with offices, maybe a car? The jeep came to a halt in front of what I can only describe as a ruined shack. The door was ill fitting and much of the roof was made up of what looked like leftover bits of wood and tin sheeting.

"We are here," my guide informed me, smiling at my obvious surprise.

I had no idea what to expect. Surely no one lived here? As we approached the entrance to the Chief's home, my guide knocked on the door. Very gently the door opened, revealing an elderly smiling gentleman. Pulling the door as far open as possible, he ushered us in.

"Thank you so much for seeing me," I blustered, trying not to appear too shocked at the state of the interior of the single room. Two chairs, a rough table and a mat on

the floor with a few boxes piled in a corner and that was it. Nothing else.

I explained who I was and why I had come. He knew all about me. Obviously no issues of communication in this nation! I was amazed. He asked about my country, the government and what I thought about the state of the British people.

Pleasantries over, I dared to approach the issue of poverty on the reservation, hoping that he did not misinterpret my question as a judgement on the state of his home.

"We are in great danger. Our young people have lost hope. This is my greatest challenge as the leader of my people, how to keep hope alive in their hearts. Without it our spirit grows weak and we will perish."

No reference to material goods, or power, but straight to that essential life-giving spirit that keeps a people alive: hope.

He caught my wandering mind, which was too afraid to ask the question: Why did his people leave him in such a poor state?

Suddenly he laughed out loud and said, "Tell me what is in your heart."

This man was seriously disarming! Trying not to blush, I said, "Chief, what can we do to help you? You seem to have so little in the way of basic furniture, heating and light, and how on earth do you manage in the winter months?" (New York State often freezes over in the winter with mountains of snow and sub-zero temperatures rarely experienced in the UK.)

Instead of being offended, he simply smiled.

"I am the Chief, the leader of my people, therefore if anyone is in need, they must come to me first and I must give them something from my own possessions. Only then can they go to the rest of the community for help."

I was stunned! What on earth could he give?

Before I could say another word, he continued, "As Chief I must be the poorest person in the nation, because I am their guardian and protector."

He could see the shock on my face. Hesitatingly, I asked, "Supposing the Chief didn't think he had anything to give, what would happen then?"

His piercing eyes took on an unnerving intensity as he said, "Then the grandmothers would call a meeting and have him removed from office. It is the grandmothers who ensure that I keep the spirit of our people alive, they are the guardians, the keepers of the vision."

"Why the grandmothers?" I asked.

"Because they are the elders, the givers of life, and they are the ones who have wise hearts when it comes to looking after their children and their children's children."

As we prepared to leave, there was so much I wanted to ask, but was afraid for fear of appearing foolishly ignorant. This man could hear and speak without words. Just before we drove away he smiled, took my hand and said, "The same Spirit speaks in both our hearts. The question is, are we brave enough to heed its calling?"

I had no doubts about the Chief, but his witness to radical humility and poverty for the sake of the common good left me wondering what would happen if our government operated under the same guardians and keepers of the vision, not to mention the Church?

This witness to a radical, sacrificial service for the common good serves as an example of what we as governors are called to be and do for our school communities. Why? Because in Christ we see the model that asks for nothing less.

In 2014 the Catholic Bishops of England and Wales released a document, *Catholic Education in England and Wales*, in which they stated:

Education is central to the mission of the Catholic Church. Since 1850, the Church's aim has been to provide a place in a Catholic school for every Catholic child.[1]

[1] Catholic Bishops' Conference of England & Wales, *Catholic Education in England and Wales* (2014), www.catholiceducation.org.uk.

The success of the mission to provide a Catholic education for all is now seen in the fact that in England and Wales the Catholic Church has:

- 1,811 primary schools
- 377 secondary schools
- 49 all-age schools
- 798,687 pupils
- 48,234 teachers
- 15 sixth form colleges
- 4 universities
- 13 university colleges and higher education institutions.

We have travelled a long way and, as the following data demonstrate, Catholic schools are in the main very successful.

How well are Catholic schools performing?

The Department for Education official statistics from Ofsted 2013–14 demonstrate that Catholic schools are outperforming the national average in examination results.

At age eleven, pupils in Catholic schools in England outperform the national average English and Maths SAT scores by an increase of 5%. At age sixteen, GCSE results, pupils in Catholic schools outperform the national average by 5%. 82% of Catholic primary schools and academies have Ofsted grades of good or outstanding. This is in comparison to a national average of 79%.

Catholic schools inclusive and diverse

- 18.4% of pupils at Catholic maintained primary schools live in the most deprived areas compared with 13.8% nationally.
- 17.3% of pupils at Catholic maintained secondary schools live in the most deprived areas compared with 12.2% nationally.
- 34.5% of pupils in Catholic maintained primary schools are from ethnic minority backgrounds compared with 28.5% nationally.
- 30.2% of pupils in Catholic maintained secondary schools are from ethnic minority backgrounds compared with 24.2% nationally.

In Wales the national census reported that the proportion of pupils of minority ethnic origin in primary schools was 9.3% and 7.5% in secondary schools. 24% of pupils from Catholic primary schools are of minority ethnic origin. This figure stands at 17.5% for Catholic secondary schools – higher than the national average, which is 24.2%.

However, there is still much to be done and even though our standing in the world of education is impressive, there can be no room for complacency because the mission before us as governors is a much more challenging one.

Catholic education endeavours to make the person of Jesus Christ known and loved, and to place Him and the teachings of the Catholic Church at the centre of the educational enterprise. In placing "Christ at the Centre", Catholic education seeks to invite all into a life of discipleship within the Body of the Church.

Catholic Education in England and Wales

Governors/directors – guardians of the vision

After four decades of either working in an advisory capacity with governors or being a member of a governing body myself, I have realised that the greatest need many have today is being able to articulate what it is that they are actually there to guard, promote and transmit. How often do we hear our fellow governors say, "We are a Catholic school and therefore we should act in a particular way"? Yet for many it is not so clear. What exactly is it to be a governor of a Catholic school? What is the vision that so many refer to but can't actually articulate in language that most of us can understand? Christopher Storr has written an excellent book entitled *Serving Two Masters? Catholic School Governors at Work* (Gracewing, 2011). This is an important academic work, which is helpful for those who would like to deepen their understanding of the development of governance of Catholic schools.

However, for the purposes of this book we will endeavour to make each chapter accessible and designed in such a way that you can use the material for personal reflection and training purposes.

The vision

The vision is not a document, policy or even a book. Quite simply it is the person of Jesus Christ!

Christ, therefore, is the teaching-centre, the model on whom the Christian shapes his [or her] life.[2]

This is very simple on the one hand and yet immensely challenging on the other. Saying we are the keepers of the vision implies an affinity that goes far beyond a simple agreement that this is the way forward, or merely a set of criteria that we all buy into. No, being a keeper of the vision means this is the greatest gift that could possibly be entrusted to me and I must guard and transmit it with my whole being.

What we are seeing here is just how much God has faith in us, never mind trust! This level of faith and trust calls for a response on our behalf. In becoming a governor in a Catholic school we are entering into a relationship, not just on a professional basis with the school, but as a response to an invitation from our Creator to work at a deeper level. Governors generally agree that they are appointed to ensure that their school is the very best it can possibly be. The challenge comes in trying to apply this desire in our daily governance of the school and in how we relate what we do, think, decide as governors to the bigger picture of why the school is here in the first place.

In the main, governors are well versed in what their role entails with respect to their legal duties. In a Catholic school this includes being the employer, a duty of care for both pupils and staff, responsibility for the curriculum, admissions, the budget and buildings, all of which come under the guidance and monitoring of the governing body. In the past training has been readily available through local authorities, and more recently through many of the independent agencies springing up in the wake of the government initiative to drastically scale back the provision available to schools within the local authority. However, help to understand the canonical requirements of governance is less widely provided for and in some areas governors find themselves very much alone, increasingly relying on the priest governor, if they have one, or on the head teacher.

How do we translate the vision into reality as a governor in a school today?

In order to do this we need to go back to the starting point of our faith, the Trinity. This is the most difficult Christian belief to understand and yet it is also the cornerstone of our faith. The word "trinity" has its origins in the Latin for "three", and the study of the Holy Trinity is about the relationship between the three "persons" (as they are known by the Church) – God the Father, God the Son and God the Holy Spirit. The big question about the Trinity concerns the relationship between these three persons and their relationship in turn with humanity. It is this aspect of relationship and our place in it that we need to focus on as governors. The very moving story of Abraham and Sarah resting in the sweltering heat of the noonday sun at the Oak of Mamre gives us a glimpse of this relationship and God's longing to be part of our lives (Genesis 18:9-15).

[2] Sacred Congregation for Catholic Education, *The Catholic School* (1977), 47.

Desert dwellers have more sense than to go visiting in the middle of the day. So we find Abraham resting in the shade waiting for the cool of the later hours. Through the haze of the heat Abraham suddenly sees three men. What follows is deeply touching. Abraham springs into action, rushes out to meet the travellers and beseeches them to take shelter and rest with him. Eastern hospitality at its best! So as not to overwhelm them and risk losing their company, he entices the men with a humble offering of just a small something to eat and drink, a little water to wash and time to rest in the shade of the tree. To Abraham's delight they agree. Having secured their acceptance, Abraham rushes to his wife Sarah and sets in motion preparations, not for humble fare but for a feast fit for a king!

Returning to his guests, Abraham waits patiently while they rest and enjoy their meal. His humility is captivating. He treats these guests as if they were indeed royalty; they become for him the centre of his universe. Having refreshed themselves, the guests begin to question Abraham. They appear not only to know him but to know the name of his wife too. The extraordinary revelations that follow leave both Abraham and Sarah in shock. Abraham falls on his face and laughs out loud whilst Sarah, eavesdropping from inside the tent, manages to laugh more discreetly. Both responses are heard by the visitors and challenged with a rhetorical question: "Is anything too difficult for the Lord?" Now they know!

This beautiful story demonstrates God's longing to be part of our life and yet not frighten or overwhelm us, so the Lord comes gently, by appearing in human form. Abraham is able to connect with his guest. What we are witnessing is God's desire for intimacy, to be part of us and our lives. God made man is in this account a visitor, a guest. Such is the humility of our God. Thousands of years later we see the very same longing of God to be at one with us, to reconcile his people to one another and to himself in the person of Jesus Christ, God made man, in the incarnation.

God comes in the person of Jesus Christ to show us how to be fully human and to become the person God created us to be:

God so loved the world that he gave his only Son.

John 3:16

This love is freely given. We are free to accept or reject it. What won't change is God's unconditional love for us, which in Jesus Christ is not only unconditional but sacrificial. He gives everything that a person can give and then gives more, proving his love for all people.

...suffered under Pontius Pilate,
was crucified, died and was buried;
he descended into hell;
on the third day he rose again from the dead.

Apostles' Creed

These are the truths that we are the keepers and guardians of. Christ loves us that much! Christ sums up the whole of the Jewish Law in his summary of the commandments:

"You shall love the Lord your God with all your heart, and with all your soul, and with all your mind." This is the greatest and first commandment. And a second is like it: "You shall love your neighbour as yourself." On these two commandments hang all the law and the prophets.

Matthew 22:37-40

The challenge for us is how to keep this story alive in a way that people of today in our schools can really hear and understand.

Vision into mission

What we are experiencing today is the need to translate the vision and mission of the Church in education into a new language, one our children, families and teachers can understand. It is rather like the challenge a musical director faces with a great opera. The words remain the same; what changes is the way in which the music is presented, so that it connects with the time and the place. The very best producers know just how to help their artists become one with their audience in such a way that every person present in the auditorium feels that he or she is the sole focus of this production.

The mission of the Church in education is what we have been called and appointed to. You are appointed into an official ministry in the Church by the bishop, whether you have been appointed as a foundation governor or joined the governing body as a teacher, parent or representative of any other body. Yet it is more than this. Fr Timothy Radcliffe OP articulates this very powerfully when he says,

It is the primary role of leadership to articulate the call to transformation and facilitate response. This call is from the Holy Spirit and not from the leader of the Church. Its articulation is part of the prophetic dimension of the ministry of leadership.[3]

Once you come together as the people responsible for the governance of the school, you are leading a team in mission responding to the challenges of the time. Pope Francis sums this up when he says,

I dream of a "missionary option", that is, a missionary impulse capable of transforming everything, so that the Church's customs, ways of doing things, times and schedules, language and structures can be suitably channelled for the evangelization of today's world rather than for her self-preservation.

Evangelii Gaudium, "The Joy of the Gospel", 27

Pope Francis is continually calling the Church in all her activities no longer to say that we are disciples but that we are "missionary disciples". To this end he asks that we are ready, willing and open to adapt to the needs of the time:

I hope that all communities will devote the necessary effort to advancing along the path of a pastoral and missionary conversion which cannot leave things as they presently are. Mere administration can no longer be enough. Throughout the world, let us be permanently in a state of mission.

Evangelii Gaudium, 25

Why such an emphasis on being "missionary disciples"? Pope Francis is speaking to the global Church and to the whole world. However, our country is now described by sociologists as the most secular corner of Europe. We certainly need "missionaries" who are prophetic risk-takers ready to adapt the choreography when and where necessary. Governors are the "big picture" people who, with the head teacher, set the next strategic steps for the journey. Benedict XVI spoke beautifully of this during his visit to this country in 2010, in his address to young people at the "Big Assembly" held at St Mary's University College, Twickenham:

In your Catholic schools, there is always a bigger picture over and above the individual subjects you study, the different skills you learn. All the work you do is placed in the context of growing in friendship with God, and all that flows from that friendship.

[3] Quoted by Daphne Viveka RSCJ, www.stjohnofgodvocation.ie/index.php?id=1017

Know the mission

No one with any sense would set out on a highly demanding mission without first equipping themselves with as much information, knowledge and understanding as possible of what they were being asked to do. Sadly, I meet many governors who have been asked to do just that. They do their best, but in order to stay true to what they have been asked to do, governors themselves need training and formation. In some dioceses this is in short supply owing to a serious lack of resources.

Keeping our focus on Jesus Christ is essential. We are carrying on his work to build a world fit for God's children. Our second source is found in the teaching of the Church about the purpose and meaning of Catholic schools.

Hearing what the Church is saying

Over the past 125 years the Catholic Church has been speaking about the urgent importance of forming and educating young people for the good of society as a whole. The need to educate for transformation is nothing new. We are called by Jesus Christ not only to be transformed into the people God has envisioned us to be, but also to be so configured into Christ that we actually allow Christ to shine forth in us. That is why it is so important to know what the Church is saying and teaching about our mission, otherwise how can we proclaim it?

The table on pp.13-14 will help you to see continuing themes from the Church of education, formation and transformation. We begin in 1885 so that you can see the evolution in thinking and understanding, but also because it was in 1885 that Rome recognised the great lengths that the bishops of England and Wales were putting into trying to educate Catholic children. Great Britain gets a special mention!

In your country of Great Britain We know that, besides yourselves, very many of your nation are not a little anxious about religious education. They do not in all things agree with Us; nevertheless they see how important, for the sake both of society and of men individually, is the preservation of that Christian wisdom which your forefathers received through St Augustine, from Our Predecessor, Gregory the Great... As often as We think of this, so often are we deeply moved, for We love with a paternal charity that island which was not undeservedly called the Mother of Saints; and We see, in the disposition of mind of which We have spoken, the greatest hope and, as it were, a pledge of the welfare and prosperity of the British people.

Go on, therefore, Venerable Brethren, in making the young your chief care; press onward in every way your episcopal work; and cultivate with alacrity and hopefulness whatever good seeds you find: for God, Who is rich in mercy will give the increase.

Leo XIII, *Spectata Fides* 5-6

It was not until 1965, in *Gravissimum Educationis*, the Declaration on Christian Education, that a more comprehensive outline of the Church's mission in education was articulated by the Second Vatican

Council. Furthermore, the Council recognised that it would not have time to revise Canon Law and it was not until 1983 that what some call the final document of Vatican II, the *Code of Canon Law*, appeared. The main tenets of the Declaration now moved into church law, giving them an additional authority. The publication of *The Catholic School* in 1977 picked up and further developed much of the Declaration on Christian Education.

Without support from your diocese it can be difficult to know where to go for guidance on the mission of the Church in education. In the table below are some of the key documents from the Church on Christian education spanning more than 125 years. Each document acknowledges the critical role of Catholic schools. Throughout, the message has constantly been the same. Catholic schools are essential to the mission of the Church. Over the years, as each challenge threatening Catholic schools has appeared, the Church has responded, constantly restating the right to educate her young people in the beliefs and values of who they are as God's children.

Table: Key documents

Date	Document	Author	Key Concepts
1885	*Spectata Fides* Encyclical on Christian Education	Leo XIII	Importance of providing Catholic education for all Education and care for the young – "for the future condition of the state depends on the early training of its children"
1905	*Acerbo Nimis* Encyclical on Teaching Christian Doctrine	Pius X	Importance of Christian doctrine as a means to combat religious ignorance
1929	*Divini Illius Magistri* Encyclical on Christian Education	Pius XI	The educational environment defined family, church, school Supreme importance of Christian education
1965	*Gravissimum Educationis* Declaration on Christian Education	Second Vatican Council	The right of all Christians to a Christian education Mission of the Church in education The importance of schools Duties and rights of parents Different types of Catholic schools
1972	*To Teach as Jesus Did: A Pastoral Message on Catholic Education*	US Conference of Catholic Bishops	Christian message, community and service Mission of the Church The need for planning and collaboration in developing educational programmes

1977	*The Catholic School*	Sacred Congregation for Catholic Education	The Catholic school and the saving mission of the Church Centre for human formation Integration of faith, life and culture Catholic schools, service to the church, society, and mission countries.
1982	*Lay Catholics in Schools: Witnesses to Faith*	Sacred Congregation for Catholic Education	The role of lay educator in a Catholic school Synthesis of faith, culture and life Vocation rather than profession Witnesses to faith
1988	*The Religious Dimension of Education in a Catholic School*	Congregation for Catholic Education	Youth in a changing world The Catholic school is an open community Faith, life and culture Teaching of Religious Education The Christian formation process
1997	*The Catholic School on the Threshold of the Third Millennium*	Congregation for Catholic Education	Joys and difficulties Educating the human person The Catholic school at the heart of the Church Identity of the Catholic school The Catholic school at the service of the communities
2002	*Consecrated Persons and their Mission in Schools: Reflections and Guidelines*	Congregation for Catholic Education	Christ the teacher Radical response Church in communion – interface with the world Educators called to evangelise, accompany the young in a search for meaning Life as vocation The dignity of women – intercultural education Solidarity with the poor Culture of peace
2007	*Educating Together in Catholic Schools: A Shared Mission between Consecrated Persons and the Lay Faithful*	Congregation for Catholic Education	Communion in the mission of education Formation for educating together Communion for opening oneself towards others
2013	*Educating to Intercultural Dialogue in Catholic Schools: Living in Harmony for a Civilization of Love*	Congregation for Catholic Education	Culture in a plural society Culture and religion Approaches to pluralism Guidance for an intercultural approach Catholic education and intercultural dialogue The contribution and responsibility of Catholic schools

Canon Law – an important source

The word "Canon" comes from the Greek kanon, *meaning a rule or practical direction.*

Canon Law (Code 1) is the body of laws and regulations made by or adopted by the Latin Church (all the other twenty-two Churches have their own Codes) for the purposes of government of the Church and its people. The *Code of Canon Law* is published as a book but for our purposes the paragraphs most useful to governors can be found in the paragraphs, or Canons as they are called, 793-806.[4]

Our task is to educate and form young people in the truths of who they are, why they are here and where they are going. St Teresa of Avila outlines it beautifully when she says,

Christ has no body but yours,
No hands, no feet on earth but yours,
Yours are the eyes with which he looks
Compassion on this world,
Yours are the feet with which he walks
to do good,
Yours are the hands with which he
blesses all the world.

In carrying out this responsibility we are continuing the mission of the Church to educate young people to look with compassion on the world and to play their part in its transformation. Much of what St Teresa is saying links directly to the articles in Canon Law concerning education.

I will be dealing with the relevant Canon Law in Chapter 2; however, it is important to know what the Church is saying in these Canons because, together with the teaching of the Church and scripture, they are the foundation stones on which we stand and from which we carry out the mission of the Church, not to mention being extremely useful when needing to set diocesan priorities for the development of Catholic education!

Equipping the governing body for the challenge

A recent survey of governors from over seventy Catholic schools has shown that very little support is in place; and, if it is, they have not known about it.

This is my third year as a governor of a Catholic high school and there is more help available for Catholic governors this year, but nowhere near enough for the challenges we have to deal with.

I have been a governor for many years, but I can only recall one talk on our place in the mission of the Church and that was a long time ago.

The following questions are offered for you to answer individually and then pool your responses together. This will help to highlight both the strengths and areas for development concerning the whole governing body's understanding of the mission of the Church in education.

[4] *Code of Canon Law*, www.vatican.va/archive/ENG1104/__P2M.HTM

Review	My response	Support required	Who can help?
What training have I received so far in the Church's mission in education?			
Which of the church documents about Catholic education have I read?			
Have I seen the extracts from Canon Law on Catholic education?			
How often does our governing body discuss our core mission?			
How accessible do you find the documents from the Church?			
To what extent does your school mission statement accurately reflect what the school is for?			
Does the mission statement need to be revisited by the whole community?			

Action

Now pool your answers and agree together what needs to be done, when and by whom. Keep this discussion as an ongoing item on your governors' agenda at meetings.

Mission to the people of our time – focus on the pupils' questions

Before we concern ourselves too much with what we are supposed to be doing as governors regarding teaching and the formation of our pupils it is important to keep in mind a central teaching of the Church. Christ dwells in each one of our pupils. He got there long before we did. He has chosen to work in and through each one. The God in the teacher reaches out to the God in the child. It is through these relationships that our young people will come to know who they are and why they are here.

However, as governors it is important that we, as well as our teachers, are able to hear the questions that the young people actually ask rather than looking for answers to questions that they are not asking. The world is changing so fast that the issues of today are not the same as those of even the more recent past. In a good school these discussions and debates happen in all areas of learning, not just in the Religious Education lessons. Pope Francis, in addressing the Congregation for Catholic Education, said that:

... education today is guided by a changing generation, and, therefore, every educator – and the entire Church who is the mother educator – is required "to change", or know how to communicate with the young people before them.

Address to the Plenary Session of the Congregation for Catholic Education, 13 February 2014

So many questions

Young people have always been full of "big questions". While we must be faithful to educating in the beliefs and values of Christianity in the Catholic tradition, so too it is essential, if there is to be any lasting connecting between the learning and their lives, that schools engage with students' questions of purpose and meaning. Let us begin with the questions that so many young people ask in school:

- Who am I really?
- Why was I born?
- What's the point of my life?

Equally interesting for many is the big question asked by Jesus himself:

- Who do you say I am?

Without realising it, these young people, who appear in every class, are asking the key questions about why the Church is so committed to her mission in education.

It is in the knowing and the living out of our faith in Jesus Christ that we make him known. In words of Benedict XVI:

To the extent that we nourish ourselves on Christ and are in love with him, we feel within us the incentive to bring others to him: Indeed, we cannot keep the joy of the faith to ourselves; we must pass it on.

Address to Convention of the Diocese of Rome, 5 June 2006

So often I hear governors speak very movingly of their commitment to their faith and their desire to pass it on. But it always comes back to: "How do we do this today?" Frequently governors say, "It's all so different today from the way I learnt." But it is not just the way in which we were taught; much of the content is far broader, incorporating areas of study that Catholic schools rarely ventured into. As part of the leadership in a Catholic school today we need to be familiar with the issues that young people are concerned with and not be too afraid if they are not our issues.

Nourishing ourselves

The Catholic school loses its purpose without constant reference to the Gospel and a frequent encounter with Christ.

The Catholic School (1977), 55

As governors we have to ensure that time is given to just this, as individuals, but also as a governing body. Do we as governors reflect together on scripture, or writings from our tradition that help us to know Christ ever more deeply? Governing bodies usually begin and end their meetings with a short prayer or reflection, but is this really enough to sustain us in our mission? Does the governing body actually reflect together on the documents of the Church that outline the mission, its joys and challenges?

Every Catholic school teaches the pupils the same truths. You can see what the bishops of England and Wales require of schools in the teaching of the Church, in their publication *Religious Education Curriculum Directory* (Catholic Bishops' Conference of England and Wales, 2012). It is these foundational beliefs that help us as governors to be clear about our core purpose. Let's take a few of these one at a time.

Who is God?

This question comes in many forms, but it is critical to our understanding of why we are here, who we are and where we are going. There are libraries of books on just this question, but for our purposes I will take a line that our pupils can follow. God is the Creator of the universe; the source of all life; God always was, is and will be. God is love and this love is greater than anything that any of us has ever experienced. Which leads us to the next question.

Who am I?

We believe that we are all made in the image and likeness of God. However, this can appear very remote and unscientific to a young mind today. So what are we really saying?

From all time you have existed in the mind of your Creator God. How do we know that? We know that because God is love and love has to love, it has to give love, recreate in and for love; otherwise it is not love. Love cannot be kept for itself, otherwise it is not by its very nature love. At a certain point in time God took a big risk. God trusted in the potential of our parents to love as we were created to. It is in that moment of risk and faith in us that human love draws down from the mind of God the vision that is you, into the womb of your mother where you were enfleshed. Nine months later, we see that vision: you. In each one we recognise something of the Creator as well as the biological parents. The image is clear for all to see. No two are alike and each one is born carrying a unique gift the world has been waiting for since the beginning of time.

God made us to love us! As amazing as it seems, that is it. So what are we to do with that idea? Again it is simple yet very challenging. Accept it, accept the fact that God made us to love us and asks nothing of us other than that we allow God to do that. That's where our response comes in. In accepting God's love we are transformed by it and love in return. It is as if our eyes are really opened for the first time and we see each other as family, brothers and sisters, one flesh and one body. Echoing some of the great themes of Vatican II, we are the people of God. We are the body of Christ. We are called to live in communion with our God and with one another.

Why am I here?

Why are we here in this school? To discover who you are – God's own children, carrying a gift the world is waiting for. Through their education it is hoped that our pupils will discover something of this gift and learn how to develop it until such time that they are called forth to give it. So often our young people do not believe that they are special, unique or worthy. Psychologists tell us that the human mind deals with approximately eighty thousand thoughts each day, of which 70% are negative! The world of advertising has become so skilled in getting exposure to the human mind that it now works on the basis that the mind picks up at least sixteen thousand messages a day. And what are these messages? "You need this product, or that gadget, because you are clearly deficient without it." Sadly, it works. Our mission is to teach the children to discern what is real and of value; to show another way that brings lasting joy and fulfilment in communities of learning and formation. Our schools must be places where young people will develop a passion for truth and justice for everyone as stewards committed to equality and respect for all God's creation. Our challenge is to continue to make this world fit for our children. Nothing less. In words of Benedict XVI:

> *The Church's mission, in fact, involves her in humanity's struggle to arrive at truth.*
>
> Address at meeting with Catholic educators, Washington DC, 17 April 2008

Where am I going?

That depends on what we choose. Our journey on earth is one of freedom. We are created in love, for love. However, love leaves the beloved free. The really challenging part of this is that God will not force us to love him or one another. We have to choose to love. Christ came as "the way, the truth and the life" to show humankind how to love. His promise to us was:

In my Father's house there are many dwelling-places. If it were not so, would I have told you that I go to prepare a place for you? And if I go and prepare a place for you, I will come again and will take you to myself, so that where I am, there you may be also.

John 14:2-3

Taking up the mission

The role of the governor as guardian of the vision has never been more important than it is today.

Their importance [Catholic schools] is in fact greater now than ever before.

To Teach as Jesus Did (1972), 84

And furthermore:

The function exercised by the school in society has no substitute; it is the most important institution that society has so far developed to respond to the right of each individual to an education and, therefore, to full personal development; it is one of the decisive elements in the structuring and the life of society itself.

Lay Catholics in Schools (1982), 13

The Catholic Church has long seen and knows full well the importance of the school not just for the Church but for the whole of society, which is why she proclaims:

The absence of the Catholic school would be a great loss for civilisation and for the natural and supernatural destiny of man.

The Catholic School (1977), 15

As governors we need to be confident in speaking with and to our world. Knowing the teaching of the Church regarding education strengthens our confidence in knowing where to go and above all not to be too daunted by the many uphill struggles.

Like the mission and message of Jesus Christ, the Church's educational mission is universal – for all men, at all times, in all places. In our world and in our nation, the mission of Christian education is of critical importance. The truth of Jesus Christ must be taught; the love of Jesus Christ must be extended to persons who seek and suffer.

To Teach as Jesus Did (1972), 15

Governors are busy people and time is often at a premium; however, it is important to know how to educate each generation for its time. Many governors have their own children in school. But what worked when we were in school, or even ten years ago, will not necessarily work today. It is in this area of knowing and understanding the pupils, as well as the staff, that governors need the guidance of the head teacher and staff.

And so, now as in the past, the Catholic school must be able to speak for itself effectively and convincingly. It is not merely a question of adaptation, but of missionary thrust, the fundamental duty to evangelize, to go towards men and women wherever they are, so that they may receive the gift of salvation.

The Catholic School on the Threshold of the Third Millennium, 3

Seeing our children, young people and staff with the eyes of Christ is the challenge. When all is going well this appears pretty straightforward, but when the opposite is the case it is quite another matter, especially as we strive to remember that our task calls for the Catholic school to engage in transformational education with the aim of inspiring transformational practice.

Reflection

To "really see" someone, especially someone who looks up to you,
is to give that person an important blessing.
In a gaze of recognition, of understanding,
in an appreciative look, there is deep blessing.
Often it is not important
that we say much to those for whom we are significant,
but it is very important that we see them.
. . . Good kings and queens see their people;
good parents see their kids;
good teachers see their students; good priests see their parishioners;
good coaches see their players; good executives see their employees;
and, in really good restaurants, the owner comes round to the tables and sees his or her customers
and the customers are, without being able to explain why,
grateful that the owner took time and pain to see them.
We are blessed by being seen.
. . .Today the young are not being seen enough in this way.
Our youth are acting out in all kinds of ways
as a means of getting our attention.
They want to, and they need to, be seen by us – parents, adults, teachers, priests, coaches, leaders.
They need our blessing.
They need to see, right in our eyes, the radical acceptance of their reality,
and they need to read in our eyes the words:
"You are my beloved child; in you I am well pleased."
Young people need our appreciative gaze;
mostly they simply need our gaze – period.
One of the deepest hungers inside young people
is the hunger for adult connection,
the desire to be recognised, seen, by a significant adult.
They desperately need, and badly want,
the blessing that comes from our gaze and presence.
They need for us to see them.
In the end, more than they want our words, they want our gaze.

Attributed to Fr Ron Rolheiser at http://roypetitfils.com/2009/10/really-seeing/

As governors we are often challenged at a very deep level and none more difficult than when we are presented with a young person who has gone off the rails and for whom there appears to be no way out. The poem below illustrates very well the struggle that so many people have in differentiating between the person and their actions.

No one else can see the beauty
In his darkened life now.
His image has closed
Like a shadow.
When people look at him

He has become the mirror
Of the damage he has done.
But he is yours;
And you have different eyes
That hold his yesterdays
In pictures no one else remembers:
He is yours in a way
No words could ever tell;
And you can see through
The stranger this deed has made him
And still find the countenance of your son.

From "For the parents of one who has committed crime" by John O'Donohue

REFLECTION POINTS

- How do you feel personally about what you have taken on?
- What is your response to the first reflection above? To what extent does it challenge you in your role?
- How do you feel about the poem by John O'Donohue?
- In reflecting on the two pieces for reflection, what questions do they pose for you personally?
- Does your governing body have a nominated person for continuing professional development, and if so are there areas you need to include in the ongoing training of the governors that are missing or underdeveloped?

CHAPTER 2

Standing on firm foundations

To accomplish great things we must not only act, but also dream, not only plan, but also believe.

Anatole France

Governors across the country are in many ways the backbone of our educational system. The many hours of work and high levels of responsibility for the well-being and support of their school communities are unprecedented in any other field. The long list of governor responsibilities varies from school to school. It is not my intention to list all the many duties of governors that are well documented in your governor's handbook and on your diocesan website. What I hope to do is explore with you how governors in a Catholic school, regardless of their status, can best support their school as it strives to become the radical, prophetic learning community it was set up to be.

To begin we need to know the legal footing that supports us. Let us look briefly at some key documents and what they are actually saying. All Catholic schools have a dual responsibility to both Church and State because they must be aware and accountable not only to the law of the land but also to requirements of the 1983 *Code of Canon Law*. Don't be put off by references to Canon Law. You will find it surprisingly easy to read and remarkably clear.

Code of Canon Law[1]

Although we have dwelt briefly with this in Chapter 1, it is very important that governors are aware of the guidance that is available to them through the Church's teaching office. It is not uncommon to see eyes glaze over the moment someone launches into the topic of Canon Law! However, this is not something just for clergy and seminarians. You may be surprised to know that Canon Law touches on many aspects of our daily living of the faith, which is why it is so important for governors. The *Code of Canon Law* devotes one of its seven books to the field of Catholic education.

Have a look at the brief outline of some key extracts that refer to education and Catholic schools. They are very supportive of what we are all trying to achieve.

Canon 747

§1 It is the obligation and inherent right of the Church, independent of any human authority, to preach the Gospel to all peoples…

[1] Quotations from Canon Law in this publication are taken from Canon Law Society of Great Britain and Ireland, *The Canon Law: Letter and Spirit* (London: Geoffrey Chapman, 1995).

§2 The Church has the right always and everywhere to proclaim moral principles, even in respect of the social order, and to make judgements about any human matter in so far as this is required by fundamental human rights or the salvation of souls.

These are strong words. They recognise that there will be times when the Church and the State will not agree. However, despite the challenges and the difficult times that ensue when there is a conflict between Church and State, the Church's right to educate her children comes from God, not the State. This is affirmed by the Second Vatican Council when it declares that the teaching office of the Church is one of the three functions for which Christ created her.[2]

Canon 795

Education must pay regard to the formation of the whole person, so that all may attain their eternal destiny and at the same time promote the common good of society. Children and young persons are therefore to be cared for in such a way that their physical, moral and intellectual talents may develop in a harmonious manner, so that they may attain a greater sense of responsibility and a right use of freedom, and be formed to take an active part in social life.

Education in a Catholic school is about educating the whole person, not only the pupils' academic and physical gifts; they must be educated spiritually, morally, socially and culturally. In this way the young are educated and formed to grow into the people God has created them to be. We can see why this is so important today, with so much pressure being put on teachers and children alike to excel in national tests; although these are important, if we are not careful we run the risk of seriously undermining the true meaning of education itself, which is a much bigger enterprise than examination results. Of course all children must have the very best education possible, but the Church insists that we do not educate just for the individual, but also for that individual to recognise and embrace his or her role in promoting the common good of everyone. This is where we need very skilled and highly informed teachers and leaders who know how to engage with contemporary issues and challenge where and when required.

Canon 796

§1 Among the means of advancing education, Christ's faithful are to consider schools as of great importance, since they are the principal means of helping parents to fulfil their role in education.

The role of parents as the first educators in the faith must always be encouraged. Parents seek admission to Catholic schools for a whole variety of reasons. Some come in good faith, others may be questionable. However, I have always seen this as an important moment not to be lost because it is a moment of encounter between the people of God and the Church, often after years of distance. It is

[2] See, for example, *Lumen Gentium*, Dogmatic Constitution on the Church, 25.

clear that many parents are struggling in the practice of their faith as Catholics, if by practising we mean going to Mass on Sunday. Many are what I call "ancestral Catholics" – somewhere in their past someone in the family was a practising Catholic and for a multitude of reasons their practice of the faith fell away. But the link is still there. They want the best for their children and very often they have a deep sense that it is to be found in the Catholic school. How they express this may be clumsy and not fit with our more polished, articulate definition, but it is there just the same. Placing their child into your hands is often the only way they can respond to being in touch with the Catholic Church. Our challenge is to work with them, meeting each family where they are rather than where they are not. Not placing obstacles in the way of people trying to find Christ is a theme dear to the heart of Pope Francis:

Instead of being just a church that welcomes and receives by keeping the doors open, let us try also to be a church that finds new roads, that is able to step outside itself and go to those who do not attend Mass, to those who have quit or are indifferent.

Interview with Fr Antonio Spadaro, August 2013

Canon 797

Parents must have a real freedom in their choice of schools. For this reason Christ's faithful must be watchful that the civil society acknowledges this freedom of parents and, in accordance with the requirements of distributive justice, even provides them with assistance.

With the loss of local authority funding for travel to the nearest Catholic school many parents are finding it financially difficult to send their children to a Catholic school. Some schools have been very creative and responded by joining together to bus children from outlying areas. However, the need to be proactive in the political sphere is never far from the door of governors of faith schools and something we should not shy away from. Governors have considerable influence and power. Don't be afraid to unite and use it!

Canon 800

§1 The Church has the right to establish and to direct schools for any field of study or of any kind and grade.

§2 Christ's faithful are to promote catholic schools, doing everything possible to help in establishing and maintaining them.

The Church has the right to establish Catholic schools where she feels there is a need, and she calls upon her entire people to strive to promote their schools. Here we find many challenges. Most Catholic schools are in the top percentile of good or outstanding schools in the country. However, there are some that are struggling and where Catholic parents are not supporting them. This is understandable as parents must choose the best possible school for their children; they deserve nothing less. However, as governors we have a call to respond as soon as possible if a neighbouring Catholic school is showing signs of getting into difficulty.

It has become common practice for schools that are flourishing to reach out to struggling schools by seconding their head teacher and/or key lead members of staff to go and help. It is important to remember that as governors we are there to support the bishop in his responsibility to educate and form our young people. It is sometimes necessary for the bishop to ask governors to move from one school to another to help turn a school around. All of these are ways in which we work for the common good and not just for our own school.

Canon 802

§1 If there are no schools in which an education is provided that is imbued with a Christian spirit, the diocesan Bishop has the responsibility of ensuring that such schools are established.

The Catholic community has a long history of digging deep into its pockets to establish a school where there are none. Today this is just as challenging, as the costs of building a new school run into many millions. However, it is the duty of a bishop to see that a school is provided. How to do it is the challenge!

Canon 803

§1 A catholic school is understood to be one which is under the control of the competent ecclesiastical authority or of a public ecclesiastical juridical person, or one which in a written document is acknowledged as Catholic by the ecclesiastical authority.

§2 Formation and education in a catholic school must be based on the principles of catholic doctrine, and the teachers must be outstanding in true doctrine and uprightness of life.

§3 No school, even if it is in fact catholic, may bear the title "catholic school" except by the consent of the competent ecclesiastical authority.

All schools that bear the title "Catholic" may do so only under the authority of the bishop. This means that they must comply with the necessary requirements that define a school as Catholic. These apply to personnel appointments as well as the provision for Religious Education, the curriculum and Catholic life of the school. Appointing the very best people for the key roles in a Catholic school is essential if the school is to be faithful to its mission.

Canon 804

§1 The formation and education in the catholic religion provided in any school, and through various means of social communication, is subject to the authority of the Church. It is for the Bishops' Conference to issue general norms concerning this field of activity and for the diocesan Bishop to regulate and watch over it.

§2 The local Ordinary is to be careful that those who are appointed as teachers of religion in schools, even non-catholic ones, are outstanding in true doctrine, in the witness of their Christian life, and in their teaching ability.

As we have already mentioned, what is to be taught in Religious Education is laid down by the bishops of England and Wales in the *Religious Education Curriculum Directory*. The bishops also insist that a minimum of 10% (5% in sixth forms) of teaching time must be given to the teaching of RE (excluding worship and assemblies). It is important for governors to familiarise themselves with the contents of this directory so that they are aware of what needs to be taught and able to discuss with those responsible for the teaching of RE how and where it is being delivered. It is always important to ask how governors can further support this key area of learning. The actual methodology of the delivery and teaching of RE is down to the expertise of the teachers concerned under the guidance of the RE curriculum coordinator in a primary school or the head of RE in a secondary school.

Religious Education is the "core of the core" curriculum. It is the most important area of learning in the school and must have at least equal resources as English and Maths. The bishop has delegated to the governing body the responsibility of ensuring that teachers of RE are competent and "are outstanding in true doctrine, in the witness of their Christian life, and in their teaching ability".

For most governing bodies this is difficult. Because of the loss of many professional Catholic teacher-training colleges, finding a teacher with this expertise is like fishing in an ever-shrinking pond. However, it is essential that we do either find them or train our own. I have been very impressed by the creativity of some schools situated in hard-to-staff areas that are doing just this. They have identified Catholic teachers with the potential to be good RE teachers and are training them in-house and with the help of their diocese.

Canon 805

In his own diocese, the local Ordinary has the right to appoint or to approve teachers of religion and, if religious or moral considerations require it, the right to remove them or to demand that they be removed.

At first reading this seems very draconian. However, the bishop is responsible for the teaching and formation of the people in his diocese. Therefore it follows that in extreme cases, after consultation with the head teacher and governors, he does have the authority to ask the governors to remove a teacher from teaching RE. Naturally one would hope that the governors would have a very close eye on the quality and delivery of Religious Education in their school and if they became aware of someone who was not fit for purpose would be in discussion with the head teacher as to the best way forward. Very often what may be needed is more training and/or support from a specialist.

Canon 806

§1 The diocesan Bishop has the right to watch over and inspect the catholic schools situated in his territory, even those established or directed by members of religious institutes. He has also the right to issue directives concerning the general regulation of catholic schools; these directives apply also to schools conducted by members of a religious institute, although they retain their autonomy in the internal management of their schools.

§2 Those who are in charge of catholic schools are to ensure, under the supervision of the local Ordinary, that the formation given in them is, in its academic standards, at least as distinguished as that in other schools in the region.

We will be looking at the whole area of inspection later, in Chapter 7. However, the second paragraph of Canon 806 sets a very high bar! It has never been acceptable for Catholic schools to be anything other than as good in academic standards as other outstanding schools in their area. Why? The answer goes back to our belief about who these children are, why they are here and where they are headed. They are God's children, made in God's image and likeness; they carry a gift the world waits for and urgently needs, and it is our task to help them find it and educate them to know how to use it as they head home – back to their Creator God.

The Trust Deed of the diocese

This is a key legal document and from time to time you will hear representatives of the diocese referring to it. You may be surprised to discover that it actually says very little about schools but deals in the main with the management of finances, assets and the estate of the trustees. However, you will see a statement that refers to the "maintenance or advancement of the Roman Catholic religion". Some dioceses do have a short reference to schools but no more than a sentence or two. These brief statements provide the legal basis for all that is done in the name of Catholic education at every level. It is for this purpose that governors are appointed – the "advancement of the Roman Catholic religion". This seems a rather broad statement, but it is meant to be, because the whole of the educational project of the Church is about just this. Put into everyday language, it means proclaiming the Good News of Jesus Christ, and educating our young people in what this means for them today in accordance with the teachings of the Catholic Church.

The Instrument of Government

Every school/college has this document. If you have not seen it, ask for a copy. It is very challenging and contains an important clause that outlines how the school must be run:

The school was founded by and is part of the Catholic Church. The school is to be conducted as a Catholic school in accordance with the Canon Law and teachings of the Catholic Church, and in accordance with the Trust Deed of the diocese of (name of diocese or religious order/congregation)… and in particular:

(a) religious education is to be in accordance with the teachings, doctrines, discipline and general and particular norms of the Catholic Church;

(b) religious worship is to be in accordance with the rites, practices, discipline and liturgical norms of the Catholic Church; and at all times the school is to serve as a witness to the Catholic faith of Our Lord Jesus Christ.

The first paragraph is quite straightforward and simply underlines the legal status of the school from both the statutory and canonical points of view.

Paragraph (a) makes it clear that the teaching of religious education must fulfil that which is laid down by the bishop. For our purposes that is outlined in the Religious Education Curriculum Directory. Few governors are aware of this very important document.

Paragraph (b) in its first sentence refers to a wide area under the heading of religious worship. This asks governors to ensure that staff are properly trained and equipped to know how to educate and enable children and young people to learn about worship, liturgy and prayer.

The final part of this second paragraph is the most challenging of all. Notice the language: "at all times" – not just in RE lessons or during assemblies, but in everything – "to serve as a witness to the Catholic faith of Our Lord Jesus Christ". This is not easy. It is, however, part of our Instrument of Government and not an optional extra for the more pious members of the school community. It is for everyone who is part of the school. The challenge is obvious, and responding to and living this out needs a good deal of help, guidance and support.

The appointment of foundation governors

You may well ask why we need foundation governors if we are all committed to the same cause. It is a very good question. Foundation governors must be practising Catholics who are fully committed to their faith in the Church and Jesus Christ. Having looked at the Instrument of Government above, you can see that the bishop needs to appoint enough people to be able to support the whole governing body as they strive to make this a reality in their school. It is a long journey! That is why foundation governors form the majority of members of the governing body, to carry out the mandate entrusted to them by the bishop and safeguard the mission.

As other members of the governing body are elected or appointed through different avenues, they may or may not be Catholic or secure in their commitment to Catholic teaching. Hence the careful appointment by the bishop (or, in the case of schools owned and run by Religious orders, the appointed person for the order) of foundation governors is necessary to ensure the Catholic nature of the school. (Academies have a different structure; however, the responsibility to comply with the requirements for Catholic education is the same.) Usually all governors are very committed and wanting to get it right. Once the whole governing body comes together they work as one united body.

Are foundation governors more important than the rest of the governing body?

No. All governors share in this responsibility as a corporate body. The reason why there are a variety of avenues through which governors are appointed is to ensure that the governing body has a wide range of expertise and skills that can be called upon to govern the school. Only the Chair in exceptional circumstances can act alone without consulting the rest of the governing body beforehand. However, the Chair must discuss any such emergency measures as soon as possible with the rest of the governing body.

The ethos statement

The law as regards the duty of the governors to secure an ethos statement is found in the Instruments of Government in the School Standards and Framework Act 1998 Schedule 12, paragraph 1:1, section (g) ("where the school is a foundation or voluntary school which has a religious character"). All schools that have a religious character must have an ethos statement. This forms part of the Instrument of Government and is quoted above in the section "The Instrument of Government".

What do we mean by "ethos"?

This is one of the terms that many governors and teachers in Catholic schools find difficult to put into clear terms. The word "ethos" comes from a Greek word for custom or habit. Simply put it is a way of living, behaving and doing things by people who, though diverse, follow common values, beliefs and vision of life. A Catholic school's ethos is seen in the many ways in which this common set of beliefs, values and vision are put into action and witnessed to in daily life. The Catholic Education Service's book Christ at the Centre (2012) defines "ethos" in this way:

A Catholic school's "ethos" may be understood to be the outward signs and experiences of the teachings of Christ and the Catholic Church in the totality of daily life in a Catholic school. (6)

It is not uncommon during headship interviews that candidates are asked to say how they would define the difference between working in a Catholic school and one that is not Catholic. A common reply is something like: "Well, it is in everything we do, our relationships and the way people are treated..."

Then so often they get stuck!

Governors need to help one another with a clear articulation of the Catholic ethos of their school. Our interviewee is right up to a point, but that does not help us much.

We need to start in the right place. Which takes us back to the question, "What is the vision of the Church in Catholic education?" Remember, it is not a policy; it is Jesus Christ, God made man. A person.

Therefore everything we are and witness to has to be consistent with our commitment to the personal experience of the teachings of Christ and the Catholic Church in the daily life of the Catholic school.

The final statement in both the Instrument of Government and the ethos statement is, as we have already seen, extremely challenging:

and at all times the school is to serve as a witness to the Catholic faith of Our Lord Jesus Christ.

This can sometimes be where governors feel they fall short. It's not surprising, we all do. What is important to remember is that as governors this is what we are striving for. Does this let us off the hook? Not at all, but it serves to recognise that when we are challenged or realise that we have failed, or made the wrong decision, we have to be ready and willing to acknowledge our failure, do something about it and then be committed to learning from this. We are all learning and it is never easy. The only real mistake is the one we don't learn from. Governors must be encouraged by the words of Pope Francis, who is not afraid to admit to his failings:

I am a sinner. This is the most accurate definition. It is not a figure of speech, a literary genre. I am a sinner.

Interview with Fr Antonio Spadaro, August 2013

What else are governors accountable for?

As we have seen, governors, along with the head teacher and senior leadership team, have a crucial role in ensuring the school is successful in meeting the needs of all its pupils and achieving high standards (Education Act 2002). They are also to ensure the well-being of pupils at the school, promote community cohesion and to work in close collaboration with parents and carers. All of these responsibilities are clearly outlined and developed in the *Governors' Handbook* (Department for Education, September 2014, 1.2):

In all types of schools, governing bodies should have a strong focus on three core strategic functions:

a. Ensuring clarity of vision, ethos and strategic direction;

b. Holding the headteacher to account for the educational performance of the school and its pupils; and

c. Overseeing the financial performance of the school and making sure its money is well spent.

Governors as employers

This is one of the most important responsibilities of the governing body. Of critical importance is the appointment of the head teacher. This is the one time when, if possible, every governor needs to be part of the process of appointment. When this appointment goes wrong, everything else runs into trouble! Those appointed to the posts of head teacher, deputy head teacher, teachers responsible for leading RE and lay chaplains must all be practising Catholics. As we have seen in the *Code of Canon Law*, governors are looking for teachers who are ready and able to support the mission of the Church in education. Governors in Catholic schools are the employers of the staff, both teaching and support staff. Some staff may be employed through a service agreement with an outside body. However, it is still the responsibility of governors to ensure that these staff are fit for purpose in a Catholic school because:

Teachers must remember that it depends chiefly on them whether the Catholic school achieves its purposes.

Gravissimum Educationis, Declaration on Christian Education (1965), 8

Your diocese and the Catholic Education Service set out clear guidance for the appointment of staff. Appointing staff is just the beginning of the process and responsibility of the governors. Getting to know all staff – their gifts, talents, hopes and worries – is key to creating a positive and thriving school community. This can be difficult as governors often have "day jobs" too. Finding time to come into school when it is in full swing is not always easy. However, there are ways round this, such as attending key functions after school and creating special occasions for staff and governors to get to know one another socially. I discovered a simple yet highly effective way for governors to be in touch in a very large comprehensive school where it was far from easy to get to know over 120 teaching staff and a large number of support staff. One governor took it upon herself to liaise each week with the school secretary and the head teacher's PA. Whenever there was an important event in the life of an individual member of staff, she would send an appropriate card addressed to his or her home. A small gesture but one that was greatly appreciated.

In another school governors often took part in "learning walks". These involved going with the head teacher or a senior member of staff on a reflective, questioning walk around the school, focusing on a particular aspect. After each of these "walks" the governors taking part would send a letter to the staff identifying things that they had been delighted to discover and see (any queries or areas of concern must only be addressed to the head teacher in confidence). Again, it all makes a difference, and praise and thanks go a long way.

Continuing professional development for all staff is essential. But notice "all staff". The first priority is to ensure that everyone is helped to deepen his or her understanding of what it is to be part of a Catholic school and its mission. This requires training, reflection and guidance, particularly for those members of staff who may not be Catholic or Christian.

Responsibility for the curriculum

At present these are shifting sands! In maintained schools, governors have a legal responsibility for the curriculum. So how is the curriculum in a Catholic school different from any other school? What should set the curriculum apart is the context in which it is situated. This context is the values and beliefs drawn from both scripture and the teaching of the Church.

Spiritual, Moral, Social and Cultural Education

The first entitlement of the nation's children in all schools is to be spiritually, morally, socially and culturally educated (Education Reform Act 1988). So what would this look like?

What you are looking for is how links and connections are being made across all subjects raising the big questions of purpose and meaning of life. Each subject leader is responsible for identifying moments or interventions when these areas or questions may be raised and explored.

Examples

Year 4 Literacy

The class were reading the book *Homecoming* by Michael Morpurgo. This is a very moving short story of a man who returns to his childhood home after fifty years of absence. The story raises many justice issues about prejudice, conservation and the environment.

As the children finished listening, the teacher asked the class to respond to the story from a variety of perspectives, thereby exploring different points of view.

As an activity the children were invited to reimagine the story, showing how they might transform the many injustices experienced by those discriminated against and protect the environment.

The teacher then challenged the class in groups to write and deliver a speech to convince the public to speak out about a local issue of injustice.

Year 9 Science

The class were researching the composition of different minerals and where they can be found. As a way of focusing the minds of the pupils the teacher had asked everyone to bring in their mobile phones for the lesson (special permission had been given as phones were not allowed in school).

The pupils were asked to place their phones on their desks and then tour the different learning areas around the room to gather information about the composition of different minerals and where they are to be found. However, what made this lesson particularly impressive was the fact that in each learning area the teacher had added some extra key facts. These all showed the impact of mining companies on the area, the exploitation of the workers and the fact that this mineral was used in the making of mobile phones. "At what price your mobile phone?" was the question.

At the end of the lesson the pupils were asked for their response to the new information that they had acquired. The final question put to the class was:

For homework I want you to write your response to someone who says to you, in the light of what you now know about mobile phones, how do you justify owning one?

In both examples you see the content of the National Curriculum being taught. What is different is the fact that moral issues are being raised and pupils are being challenged to think deeply about their learning according to Christian beliefs.

It is important to nominate a senior member of staff to have special responsibility for the area of spiritual, moral, social and cultural education so that he or she may support the less confident teachers in the delivery of Catholic teaching and how it can influence learning across the curriculum. As governors you could find it helpful to invite this person to speak to you and take you through how this is being mapped and delivered.

Admissions

Governors are responsible for drawing up and administering the admissions criteria for entry to the school. However, governors should always seek advice from the diocese before making any changes to their admissions policy. Admissions can be a very difficult area, particularly where there are not enough places for the number of Catholic children wishing to come to the school. In the cases where there simply are not enough places there can be the temptation to go down the "quantifiable avenue", defining Catholicity by adding the word "practising". This immediately leads into very difficult terrain and can end up with parents desperate to get their child further up the admissions ladder by producing a list of all the things that they do, which in their eyes puts them ahead of the next person. Or, even more worrying, the "passport system" where a register is kept of attendance at Mass!

While one has every sympathy for the frustration parents may feel at not being able to secure a place in a Catholic school, what is needed are more places. So it is back to the responsibility of the bishop to provide sufficient places for Catholic children who need them. Not easy!

Finances

Governors are responsible for drawing up an annual budget of expenditure for the school in accordance with the funding delegated by the local authority or Government and ensuring these funds are properly used. In a Catholic school, while every child must receive the very best education possible, governors are reminded that there is also the obligation to give priority to those in the greatest need:

> *...and especially in caring for the needs of those who are poor in the goods of this world or who are deprived of the assistance and affection of a family...*
>
> *Gravissimum Educationis*, 9

Pope Francis frequently calls the Church to recognise that:

> *The proclamation of the Gospel is destined for the poor first of all, for all those who all too often lack what they need to live a dignified life. To them first are proclaimed the glad tidings that God loves them with a preferential love and comes to visit them through the charitable works that disciples of Christ do in his name. Go to the poor first of all: this is the priority.*
>
> Address to Convention of the Diocese of Rome, 17 June 2013

Property

Most schools are very functional in their design; however, this should not prevent them from being places of beauty and celebration. Integral to the buildings and the environment should be expressions of the Catholic life of the school. Not every school can have a chapel, but a prayer room, or sacred space, can be created more easily, especially for key liturgical seasons of the year. Outside areas are also ideal for creating sacred spaces, prayer gardens and focal points.

Governors are responsible for the school property. They must ensure the premises are safe, without risk to the health of staff, pupils and visitors, and are as far as possible accessible for all children and staff. This can be very expensive in older buildings, which often have multiple levels, floors and endless steps. Yet with the help of the community, parish and families much can be done to see that every child is able to access his or her school. A walk round the school on a regular basis with the person responsible for health and safety will do much to help inform governors about the condition and fitness for purpose of the premises. They must also ensure that the school is adequately insured. Guidance in these matters is available from your diocese.

Meetings and getting to know your school

The days of governing bodies meeting only three times a year have long gone. Although governors are required to meet at least three times a year, in effect they meet in committees and focus groups more frequently. One of the areas I have often found to be underdeveloped is the need to have a standing item on every full governors' meeting to report on and review the Catholic life of the school. This is such a vast area that it really needs to be broken down.

A framework for a possible way forward

The following five areas of focus for the governing body are offered as a simple way of breaking down what often appears as a daunting task. Schools are very complex and multilayered. However, a useful way forward I have found is to break the task into manageable sections and focus on understanding one dimension in depth rather than everything all at once. Invite governors who are not on the same committee to work in pairs and carry out a fact-finding exploration into one of the following areas. Try to report back on your findings to the full governing body on a regular basis. Don't forget to include recommendations for any action on behalf of the governors.

Area 1. The environment Is it welcoming, bright and interesting? Is it well cared for, safe and clean throughout? Do pupils and staff show that they are proud of their school environment? Is it pupil-friendly/centred? How accessible are the school grounds and buildings for people with disabilities? Is there a dedicated area for private prayer? How does it reflect and celebrate who we are as a Catholic school? Are the classrooms interesting and good places for learning? Are the facilities for all the staff in good order and fit for purpose, comfortable, welcoming? Is there an awareness of stewardship among all staff and pupils, where everyone is responsible and accountable?

Area 2. The prayer life and worship within the school Is there a systematic and developmental programme to develop prayer and worship across the school, which draws on a wide range of Christian traditions? Is it effective and helpful? How confident are teachers and support staff in delivering this? Is there a daily act of worship and is it appropriate to the age group? Do governors pray together? Do staff have times of prayer and reflection together? How does the school help parents to pray with their children?

Area 3. Linking with the parish How does the school engage with prayer and worship in the parish (or parishes, if there is more than one)? How does your school communicate with their local parish(es), share news and join together for appropriate activities? Is the school well known in the parish(es) and do parishioners feel welcome and visit the school to support key events? To what extent are your pupils able to take an active role in the life of the parish(es) other than attending Mass or receiving the sacraments? Do pupils lead liturgies and celebrations or display appropriate exhibitions of their work in the parish(es)?

Area 4. Linking with the home How is your school supporting parents in the education of their children and in particular their religious education? To what extent are parents informed about their children's religious education and formation? How much home learning is actually being encouraged by the school and are parents able and supported in helping their children with their home learning?

Area 5. The teaching of Religious Education Ask the head teacher if you may visit some classes when RE is being taught so that you can see for yourself what is happening and how the children are responding. Is RE seen as the core of the core curriculum – the most important area of learning in the school? Talk with the teacher responsible for RE so that you have a better grasp of the RE curriculum, its strengths and weakness, and concerns that the teachers may have. Ask the staff how the governors might further support them in the teaching and delivery of RE. Discuss with the head teacher the plans for the further development of all staff in their own knowledge and understanding of Catholic teaching and scripture. Check with the teacher responsible for Continuing Professional Development that this is actually happening – if not, what can the governors do to help?

Training for governors

Ongoing training is essential for all governors. As far as governor responsibilities with respect to the State are concerned, there is much that is excellent by way of training through local authorities and national agencies. Schools are investing in training such as "Governor Mark – Quality Mark for School Governance" as a means of evaluating their own performance and effectiveness as a governing body. Another very helpful avenue is through the National College for Teaching and Leadership's training programme to become a national leader of governance (NLG). This training enables chairs of governors to use their skills and experience in supporting other chairs to improve their school or academy performance.

The training aims to help the governing body to be:

- more skilled, focused and effective
- more aware of the freedoms that it has to work in different ways
- clear in its vision for the school or academy and how, together with the school leadership team, it can achieve this
- confident that it has a clear delineation of roles and responsibilities
- staffed with the right number of skilled and committed governors to meet the needs of the school or academy.[3]

While this is extremely helpful, it naturally lacks the essential Catholic context. Therefore it is really important to try to identify chairs of governors of Catholic schools who are qualified and available in your area. By visiting **www.gov.uk/reviews-of-school-governance** you may be able to identify a suitable national leader of governance to assist you.

Dioceses are trying to provide governor training across all their schools. This should be your first point of contact. However, due to a lack of resources in some areas and the significant numbers of governors who need formation and training in the Church's mission in education, it is proving very difficult to meet the needs. Once again, there is always a creative way forward. By carrying out a review and evaluation of your governing body's effective governance and leadership you will be able to make an informed assessment of where your strengths and areas for development are. We will be looking at this in Chapter 5.

Staying on the right side of the line!

This can be tricky! Governors are the "big picture" or strategic people who

> *are the strategic leaders of our schools and have a vital role to play in making sure every child gets the best possible education.*
>
> *Governors' Handbook*, September 2014, 1.2

In the *Governors' Handbook* you will find a very helpful table in section 1.2, which clearly outlines your key responsibilities.

[3] Accessed at www.gov.uk/reviews-of-school-governance

Yes, it is true that at the end of the day the buck does stop with the governing body. However, the head teacher and the senior leadership team are there to implement the decisions concerning the direction of the school. It is not the business of the governing body to become involved in the day-to-day leadership and management of the school.

The challenge does come in how the term "critical friend" is understood. Most heads are delighted when governors ask questions, the more searching the better. This shows that they are keen to know as much as possible and really interested. A head teacher relies on the governing body to bounce ideas off and for help in finding the way forward in a fast-moving and often complex area. Take heart, Pope Francis welcomes critical friends:

I like it when someone tells me, "I don't agree." This is a true collaborator. When they say, "Oh, how great, how great, how great," that's not useful.

Press conference during return flight from World Youth Day, 28 July 2013

What is not helpful is when governors assume an expertise that they do not have and try to act on it. This usually leads to a serious breakdown in relationships and trust.

Trust is key to good and constructive leadership. No head teacher can function well without the full support of the governing body. A really helpful model for the most effective governing body is portrayed in the words of the ancient Chinese philosopher Lao-Tzu:

When the best leaders' work is done, the people say, "we did it ourselves".

Reflection

Don't try to imitate the lark or the nightingale, if you can't do it. If it's your destiny to croak like a toad, then go ahead! And with all your might make them hear you!

Louis-Ferdinand Céline

For as in one body we have many members, and not all the members have the same function, so we, who are many, are one body in Christ, and individually we are members one of another.
We have gifts that differ according to the grace given to us: prophecy, in proportion to faith; ministry, in ministering; the teacher, in teaching; the exhorter, in exhortation; the giver, in generosity; the leader, in diligence; the compassionate, in cheerfulness.
Let love be genuine; hate what is evil, hold fast to what is good; love one another with mutual affection; outdo one another in showing honour.
Do not lag in zeal, be ardent in spirit, serve the Lord. Rejoice in hope, be patient in suffering, persevere in prayer. Contribute to the needs of the saints; extend hospitality to strangers.

Romans 12:4-13

"COMETH THE HOUR, COMETH THE MAN"

During World War II, a popular legend about King Christian of Denmark was published in the American press.

King Christian X of Denmark was prone to be very autocratic and often found himself at odds not only with his people but also with his government. However, as is often the case, the old saying, "cometh the hour, cometh the man", was never more true than in the case of King Christian. According to the legend, his true leadership emerged in his people's darkest hour and Christian became the leader they needed and wanted. The Danes had protected their Jewish citizens by refusing to discriminate between Jews and non-Jews, because, as far as they were concerned, they were Danes regardless of religion.

One day King Christian saw a Nazi flag flying over a prominent hotel. He ordered a German officer to take it down and replace it with the Danish flag. The German officer refused to remove the Nazi flag. Christian pointed out that if he did not remove the flag, a Danish soldier would be sent to remove it. A high-ranking German officer stepped up and replied, "Then he shall be shot!" To which King Christian replied, "That Danish soldier will be me."

REFLECTION POINTS

- How has reading this chapter helped you to reflect on your role?
- To what extent have you encountered information that you did not know before? How confident are you in working out of this brief?
- How informed and familiar are you with the content of the teaching of religious education in your school? What do you think the governors could do to support staff and pupils in their religious education?
- How familiar are you with what is being delivered to develop the pupils' spiritual and moral education?
- Are there any ideas regarding contact with the school and getting to know it better that you and your governors might adopt?

CHAPTER 3

The challenge of forming the right team for the mission

If you want to build a ship, don't drum up people to collect wood and assign them tasks and work, but rather teach them to long for the endless immensity of the sea.

Attributed to Antoine de Saint-Exupéry

A case study

"Can you show me your log of governor training please?" asked the lead Ofsted inspector.

We froze! We didn't have one, and if we had it would have been thin. Yes, there were a few of us who tried to get to most of the important training sessions on finance, child protection and health and safety, but the rest, well, we simply never managed to attend anything else. It was not through any sense of laziness or ill will, just somehow the months went by and it didn't happen. It had never occurred to us that it might have been a good idea to have a governor who had the task of keeping us up to the mark and making sure each governor attended something of importance. We had, however, been blessed with an excellent clerk who went to endless trouble to provide us with handouts on the latest legislation, changes and updates for governors. Without this backup and our ability to convince the inspection team that we did know what we were doing, I don't think we would have escaped a grade above "requires improvement". We came out with the Ofsted grade of "good" but only just; and if that had happened today I don't think the grade would have been as high. Needless to say, the first recommendation in our report was aimed at our need to improve our governance!

As a result of this "close shave" the governors set about taking a serious look at their skills and areas for development. This led to something quite different from simply carrying out a routine skills audit as mentioned in the September 2014 Ofsted *Governors' Handbook*. The ongoing professional development of the governing body was one thing, but in revisiting the need for an audit we recognised that once again we were operating within a very superficial context, or, quite simply, the wrong one. Governors of all schools need to be skilled and professional in all areas of their governance. Governors in a Catholic school need to operate at an equally high level but with a broader perspective, which incorporates the mission of the Church in education.

Formation for ministry

The starting place for ministry in the Church has to be formation. The bishop entrusts the education and formation of young people to the governing body who delegate the day-to-day business of education to a highly skilled team of educators, led by the head teacher. When you begin with formation then the business of the governing body is seen in quite a different light. It is first and foremost a ministry in the Church, for the Church and the whole people of God.

Undoubtedly there is much that can be learnt from the local authority or training bodies for governors, but all training must clearly serve the core purpose of why governors are appointed in the first place. We need to learn skills and acquire tools for effective operations and procedures. All very necessary, but they need to be guided by beliefs and values about the importance and sacredness of the children and adults, made in the image and likeness of our God, that we are there to serve.

Formation – what is it?

When we speak of formation in the context of the Church's mission in education we are referring to spiritual formation as the process of transformation of the innermost dimension of the human being, the heart, the spirit or will. It is the ongoing process of being transformed in such a way that all thoughts, words and actions are guided by an awareness of Christ working in and through each one. A governing body that seeks to discover how God may be leading and challenging them in their role as educators of young people, responsible for their formation, who in turn are being prepared for nothing less than the transformation of society, is one that is fully in tune with the mission and goal of the Catholic Church today. But how to do this and who will help are the key questions.

Dioceses vary in their capacity to provide formation programmes for governors. Information gleaned from a recent survey of serving governors in Catholic schools revealed little or no reference to formation.[1]

There were more frequent references to Catholic ethos, but little evidence of how this impacted on the running of the school. As far as support for their roles as governors of a Catholic school went, this was at best limited to a session in the evening or one session as part of an induction day for Chairs of governors.

[1] Survey of governors of Catholic schools carried out by Redemptorist Publications, February–May 2014.

In only two dioceses was there anything more substantial, amounting to more than one session, and in only one of these two was there a full day's training focused on formation for mission.

The need is great and the resources few; however, this does not mean that there is no way forward. As we noted in Chapter 1, it is of the utmost importance that governors know and understand what it is that they are the guardians of.

Getting our priorities right

At the heart of Catholic education there is always Jesus Christ: everything that happens in Catholic schools and universities should lead to an encounter with the living Christ. If we look at the great educational challenges that we will face soon, we must keep the memory of God made flesh in the history of mankind – in our history – alive.

Congregation for Catholic Education (for Educational Institutions), "Educating Today and Tomorrow: A Renewing Passion", *Instrumentum laboris* (2014), II

As a governor I cannot give what I haven't got. The first priority of being part of the Church's mission, as Pope Francis continually reminds us, is that evangelisation is the work of God:

Though it is true that this mission demands great generosity on our part, it would be wrong to see it as a heroic individual undertaking, for it is first and foremost the Lord's work, surpassing anything which we can see and understand. Jesus is "the first and greatest evangelizer".

Evangelii Gaudium, "The Joy of the Gospel", 12

But we need to know how God is speaking to us and trying to use us as the leaven in the dough. Most of all, our own personal relationship with God has to be something that is nourished and developed. It does not happen by accident or osmosis.

How can we do this?

There are some simple yet effective steps that can be taken easily, along with the need to identify what would help you and your governors now. Taking small steps regularly may be more practical and helpful than trying to do too much too fast. Formation is an ongoing, lifelong process. The key areas of formation for your ministry as a governor of a Catholic school should include:

- Understanding what it is to be involved in Christ-centred transformational leadership
- A deepening of spiritual awareness
- Enhanced theological knowledge
- The development of pastoral and professional skills.

In some dioceses there are opportunities for governors to take advantage of all or some of these areas of formation. Sadly, there are too many where the resources are just not there. So what then? Begin where you are and with what is possible. No two people are in the same place or have the same needs. However, what is important is to make time and give the spiritual life of the governing body space to develop. The following are some simple first steps that every governing body could easily undertake.

Beginning our meetings with a quiet time of prayer and reflection

A quiet time of five to ten minutes of prayer and reflection really helps to focus all the governing body on why they are together. Chapter 8 will provide some prayers for different occasions and times of the year. But for our purposes now it is important to agree that prayer is our starting point.

It does not always have to be the Chair or the priest who prepares and leads this. What can be very good is to invite a different governor to prepare and lead the prayer for each meeting. This also includes the committees. Keep it simple and appropriate to the time and place. It may be helpful to ask the clerk to email everyone when sending the agenda out, to ask if there is anything particular that a governor may wish to ask for prayers for. This can then be passed on to the person leading the prayer.

Ending our meetings with prayer

The agenda should always allow five minutes' reflection time at the end where a governor leads a closing prayer (see Chapter 8). This enables each person to look and listen again to what God may be asking of us, especially if the way seems difficult. Again this can be a different governor from the one who led the opening prayer.

A retreat/reflection day for the governing body

A day led by a retreat giver can prove to be one of the defining moments in the life of a governing body. Taking the time to go away together to a quiet place, switching off phones and "to do" lists, makes time for God to get through to us. Our individual relationship with God needs nourishing in just the same way as any human relationship does. How often do we all hear our families or friends say to us, "You're just too busy", "We never talk any more", "Ships passing in the night"? When that happens either we do something about it or the relationship suffers and often breaks. I am amazed at the way in which places of worship fill up in times of tragedy and worry. Even those who never go to a church will stand for hours by the scene of a tragedy, with flowers and candles lit as they reflect or pray. Something deep inside each one yearns for help, understanding and connection with someone, something greater than ourselves. Hopefully, we don't wait till something drastic happens before we stop and allow God some space in our lives.

The governing body is like the powerhouse for the school. They are the ones that the head teacher can turn to for encouragement, direction and, above all, leadership. The governors are there to breathe life into the community. That life has to be the very spirit of Jesus Christ working in and through them. Pope Francis reminds us why we are on mission:

Lastly, we cannot forget that evangelization is first and foremost about preaching the Gospel to those who do not know Jesus Christ or who have always rejected him. Many of them are quietly seeking God, led by a yearning to see his face, even in countries of ancient Christian tradition.

Evangelii Gaudium, 15

We have to show that we know Jesus Christ and are passionate about him. When I lived in Watford, every Saturday hundreds of people streamed past my window heading for the football stadium, decked out in the oddest of outfits, silly tall hats, big garish rosettes, with scarfs trailing to the floor, young and old wearing the kit of their favourite player. With bold confidence they were singing their songs, telling their stories of past glorious times, living in the hope that they would add to their victories. They weren't just a crowd; they were more than that. Fans, no; more than that, too. They *were* the team. The men who competed on the pitch were just part of it. These animated streams of people were on fire! Today was always "the day". Telling the story, proclaiming who and what they were, was a major part of the day. Who could resist the joy of spreading the news that they had come to support their team? Who among them did not know every detail of their history, who scored what goal, when and where? So much excitement, commitment and enthusiasm about a game of kicking a ball around a patch of grass… or is it much, much, more?

These scenes are always a challenge to me. The supporters usually pay a goodly sum of money to go, travel great distances and spend a considerable amount of time every week in this pursuit. So what can we learn from this?

There is desire for community, to belong to something greater than ourselves, to be part of something that aspires to greatness, being the very best it is possible to be. It is the knowledge and understanding of who they are and their place in the big scheme of life in the community. It is about belonging, joy, enthusiasm, life, purpose, hunger and, above all, hope.

Our mission is to reignite just that. It is the children's inheritance and their right.

All of them have a right to receive the Gospel. Christians have the duty to proclaim the Gospel without excluding anyone. Instead of seeming to impose new obligations, they should appear as people who wish to share their joy, who point to a horizon of beauty and who invite others to a delicious banquet. It is not by proselytizing that the Church grows, but "by attraction".

John Paul II asked us to recognize that "there must be no lessening of the impetus to preach the Gospel" to those who are far from Christ, "because this is the first task of the Church". Indeed, "today missionary activity still represents the greatest challenge for the Church" and "the missionary task must remain foremost".

Evangelii Gaudium, 14

For us to know what it is we need to do requires time together and separately with God. Only then can God reveal the next steps to us. We need to immerse ourselves in our story, through scripture and the teaching of the Church. This can seem daunting, but today we are seeing a new dawn in communication coming from the Church. Pope Francis is continuing Benedict XVI's call to use all means possible to get the message out to the four corners of the earth. Pope Francis is taking it even further by using the language of the street and not the often incomprehensible language of the Church… he speaks simply, in words, yes, but most powerfully of all through his actions.

It is interesting that so many of our really inspirational leaders in the Church, who by the very nature of their responsibilities have to work tirelessly, will rise very early in the morning in order to give the first hour to prayer. Without it, they say, it simply is not possible to continue. Pope Francis challenges us again when he asks:

What would happen if we were to take these words seriously? We would realize that missionary outreach is paradigmatic for all the Church's activity. Along these lines the Latin American bishops stated that we "cannot passively and calmly wait in our church buildings"; we need to move "from a pastoral ministry of mere conservation to a decidedly missionary pastoral ministry". This task continues to be a source of immense joy for the Church.

Evangelii Gaudium, 15

Just in case you feel that it is not your place to step up, Pope Francis challenges us to be bold and not to be held back by those who say, "It can't be done," or "We have always done it this way," refusing to try something new:

I invite everyone to be bold and creative in this task of rethinking the goals, structures, style and methods of evangelization in their respective communities. A proposal of goals without an adequate communal search for the means of achieving them will inevitably prove illusory. I encourage everyone to apply the guidelines found in this document generously and courageously, without inhibitions or fear.

Evangelii Gaudium, 33

So often we feel inadequate for the task and uncertain if this is what we should be doing. These are just the times when we need to turn to the Lord for guidance and help. It is as Pope Francis says,

The important thing is to not walk alone, but to rely on each other as brothers and sisters, and especially under the leadership of the bishops, in a wise and realistic pastoral discernment.

Evangelii Gaudium, 33

Governor study days

Why not take the invitation from Pope Francis, "I invite everyone to be bold and creative," and begin by setting aside a study day with someone who can lead and guide governors in the inspirational document *Evangelii Gaudium*, "The Joy of the Gospel"? This will certainly help and hopefully inspire each one to feel re-energised and enthusiastic about their role and ministry.

Sometimes it is not easy to find the right course leader, but by contacting your diocesan education office and speaking to the person responsible for governor support you should be able to find the right person.

Self-help 1: Individual reflections

Another useful technique is to go online and look for a page that has quotes from the Church on a topic that the governors can focus on. In order to involve everyone print off a variety of quotes from either *Evangelii Gaudium*, scripture or another important text, and allocate them to each governor at least a week before you come together. Ask the governors in turn to simply say how they see this extract, their own response to it and then how they see it in relation to their shared ministry as governors. As your governing body may be large, adjust the presentations according to the time available. Leave time for silent reflection before anyone responds.

Self-help 2: Committee's reflections

Another form of the above would be to give each committee member the same extract and ask them to prepare together a presentation for the rest of the governing body. Leave time for silence and reflection. It is not always necessary to speak.

Accessing the information

"The Pope App" is free and gives you a daily running account of what is happening in the Church, what is being said as well as images, speeches and events.

Pope Francis' *Evangelii Gaudium*, "The Joy of the Gospel", can be bought, or may be downloaded from the Vatican website: **w2.vatican.va/content/francesco/en/apost_exhortations/documents/papa-francesco_esortazione-ap_20131124_evangelii-gaudium.html**

VIS, the Vatican Information Service, is an excellent site for texts as they come out. You can also search for documents according to titles: **www.visnews-en.blogspot.co.uk/**

Pope Francis Brainy Quotes is an interesting website as it will give you an extensive and wide-ranging set of quotes from Pope Francis. It is fast-moving and changes often: **www.brainyquote.com/quotes/authors/p/pope_francis.html**

Formation for head teachers

Care for and of the head teacher is of critical importance. Just as governors need to replenish their spiritual well-being, so too does the head teacher. Sadly, this is often neglected, simply because the head either does not recognise the importance of doing so, or is so busy with "other things" that this area seems to be the easiest to "let go". In doing so, heads often find it difficult to keep the radical option of the Church in education as their guiding force. As other pressures pile in and appear to be essential in keeping the school going, what in fact actually happens is that the mission can be lost, and the school merges into being no different from other schools nearby without a faith context.

Head teachers are very aware that they need to be continually on top of their game as they sometimes strive to survive. However, survival is not dependent on being just like everyone else. What we are called to be is radically different. Our first response has to be to those in the greatest need, children who are marginalised or discriminated against; children who have lost hope and are often left to their own devices with little in the way of family or friends. Or, to put it plainly, children that other schools try hard not to include. In welcoming those who are marginalised the Catholic school responds to the very heart of the Church's mission – to provide a top-quality education and formation for those who need it the most.

EducareM – Catholic head teachers and educationalists supporting Catholic heads

Over the past few years the charity EducareM has responded to this call for help from heads. Many head teachers recognised that their professional training and support were easily accessible (though often expensive), but the provision for spiritual formation and direction was thin to non-existent.

Dioceses do provide heads' conferences and a few are providing retreat days. I would go so far as to say that as governors we must ensure that the head has all the support that he or she needs to be the spiritual leader of the school. Heads sometimes feel that they are being self-indulgent in requesting this and therefore don't ask. They should not have to ask, because the governors should be asking the head how they can support and offer concrete opportunities as part of the head teacher's entitlement. Otherwise the tank runs on empty and grinds to a halt!

The Catholic Head Teachers' National Retreat

This event is offered to heads from all over the country so that they can have a short two-day retreat experience led by an inspirational retreat director. Each retreat focuses on the individual's relationship with God and invites retreatants to reflect on how God is trying to work in and through them. It is an opportunity for heads to stop, reflect, pray and recharge their batteries at the end of a busy year.

Recently head teachers have asked if they might bring a governor with them to share the experience. This has proved to be very worthwhile and as a result the retreat is now for heads and governors. For further information have a look at the website **www.educarem.org.uk/**

Spiritual direction/accompaniment for head teachers

One of the outcomes of the Catholic Head Teachers' National Retreat has been the request for personal spiritual direction and support.

What is spiritual direction?

Spiritual direction, or accompaniment as it is sometimes called, is a way of journeying with people in order to share, with a highly trained guide, how they see God working in their lives, and trying to find a way to deepen this relationship of faith so that it really is the life blood that permeates their existence. Marian Cowan CSJ, from Spiritual Directors International, says of spiritual direction:

Spiritual direction is a time-honored term for a conversation, ordinarily between two persons, in which one person consults another, more spiritually experienced person about the ways in which God may be touching her or his life, directly or indirectly…

Although spiritual direction has had a burst of new life, it is really quite ancient. Across both the Hebrew and the Christian scriptures, we find people seeking spiritual counsel. The Queen of Sheba sought out the wisdom of Solomon. Jesus gave us examples in his conversations with Nicodemus, with the woman at the well, in the ongoing formation of Peter and the other disciples. In the early Church, people flocked to hermits in the desert for spiritual counsel. Across the centuries we find striking examples in some Irish monks, in some German Benedictine nuns, in Charles de Foucauld, Teresa of

Avila, John of the Cross, Francis de Sales, and others. Today, spiritual directors come from many traditions...

Sometimes it is very difficult to see the wood for the trees, so having a skilled spiritual guide who listens to you and helps identify how God may be trying to reveal himself to you, informing your decisions, is a great help.

It is a conversation about your life in the light of your relationship with God, helping the individual to see and understand what is happening in his or her life and where it is going. In all this the real spiritual guide is, of course, God.

Head teachers' appraisal

This presents another opportunity for governors to begin in the right place by agreeing with the head teacher an area for development related to the core purpose of the school – its mission. The setting of targets is very often agreed in relation to performance that can be measured by data and exam or SATS results. Naturally these are important; however, outstanding performance comes from understanding the "why" of what we are doing. It is inspiration and motivation that ignite and inspire teachers and young people to soar. "Outstanding" can be seen as just the first level for a Catholic school; what the Church calls for is striving for excellence, which is part of the lifelong journey to perfection. Therefore the setting of all targets needs to be done in this spirit.

It is important to begin the appraisal by listening as the head tells the story of how he or she sees God moving and working in the school. These can be special moments, events that clearly indicate the movement of the Holy Spirit.

Example (reproduced with permission)

As a designated governor for my head teacher's appraisal I was very nervous, as it was the first time that I had taken part in any appraisal meeting, never mind a head teacher's. I had been on a course about what to do and had busied myself with getting the room ready. I found the appropriate chairs, and set them out. No distractions or untidiness, just water, a "Please do not disturb" notice on the door, tissues (discreetly placed!) and my file. It was not long before everyone filed in, including a rather nervous-looking head. We began. The introductions were over and the Chair launched into the review. Suddenly the head said, "Would you mind if I shared something with you?" I glanced at the tissues, hoping they would not be needed. The Chair was a little taken aback, but thank goodness she said, "No, of course not, but is it relevant?" The head ignored the question and continued:

This morning one of our children, who is well known to everyone here because we have a final hearing to decide whether she should remain in this school or not, left me a letter. I am so disturbed by what she said that I have to share it with you. We have given her repeated chances to change, supported her with counselling, and I feel we have done all we can to help her to remain here. However, I felt, until now, that we had exhausted every possible avenue and a managed transfer is the only way forward.

The pupil's letter is reproduced here without correction:

Dear Miss

I know I deserve to be sent away. I know I have done wrong stuff, loads of it. I couldnt tell anybody why thats why I am riting now. I suppose you will think I am laying it on to get let off, but im not I just want you to know. You took me in when loads of others said no. You kept giving me chances. I failed them all. Didn't want to, just did. I don't hate... I want her to be my friend but she knows about me and my issues so her mums told her to keep clear. You are the only person who said you even liked me and the only person who has ever forgiven me I usually just get slapped. I no theres no school that will have me so I have to go to the unit. I just want to say thanks for trying to love me. wont forget you. Please remember me I was good some days wasnt I?

A silence, so silent that it hurt, hung in the air as the child's words reverberated around the room. Quietly the head teacher broke into our thoughts and said: "If you don't mind I want to begin our time together asking for the Holy Spirit's guidance. My leadership of this school is not a job. Our mission statement says, 'Learning together as God's family in love and forgiveness'; I need you to review with me if I am doing that, am I really living the mission statement or is it something I pay lip service to in tough times?"

What followed didn't feature in my training by the local authority on how to conduct a head teacher's appraisal but by the end of our time together I felt that it had been a real privilege to be part of it. It wasn't just the head who ended up being appraised; I wondered if we hadn't all been reviewed.

Our head teacher had profoundly challenged our idea of appraisal. We realised that we needed to refocus our criteria, situating our questioning and choice of targets within a mission context that not only unites our common purpose but also challenges.

Reflection

THE POWER OF ONE

One song can spark a moment,
One whisper can wake the dream.
One tree can start a forest,
One bird can herald spring.

One smile begins a friendship,
One moment can make one fall in love
One star can guide a ship at sea,
One word can frame the goal

One vote can change a nation,
One sunbeam lights a room
One candle wipes out darkness,
One laugh will conquer gloom.

One step must start each journey.
One word must start each prayer.
One hope will raise our spirits,
One touch can show you care.

One voice can speak with wisdom,
One heart can know what's true,
One life can make a difference,
You see, it's up to you!

Ashish Ram

REFLECTION POINTS

- Has anything struck you in this chapter and challenged you? If so, what and why?
- How would you like to see the formation of your governing body develop?
- How are you as a governor being spiritually nourished and supported? What do you feel you need today?
- To what extent is the spiritual education and formation of all pupils and staff a priority in your school? How might this be further developed?
- Are you as a governing body caring for the spiritual well-being of your head so that the head can carry out his or her role to the full?

CHAPTER 4

People of innovation, challenge and change

Choosing to act on what matters is the choice to live a passionate existence, which is anything but controlled and predictable.

Peter Block

There is a wonderful scene in Lewis Carroll's *Alice in Wonderland* where Alice comes to a fork in the road. "Which one will I take?" she asked. "Where do you want to go?" responded the Cheshire Cat. "I don't know," Alice answered. "Then", said the cat, "it doesn't matter." It summarises so well how we can become so lost in our surroundings that we really don't know which way to turn. So we simply "plod on", hoping that we won't go too astray. Then suddenly we come into a clearing and we see possibilities never imagined before. These are the defining moments in any school's life, when the leadership has the courage to "Go where no one has ever gone before and leave a trail." In this chapter I would like to share some examples of dioceses, governors and head teachers who have taken considerable risks to do things differently simply because they have found themselves at a crossroads and have not known which way to go. Their next steps were all based on having a clear idea of what they were trying to achieve and where they wanted to go. It was the question of "how to get there" that was so difficult. I would like to consider some of these issues facing governors today and offer a few guidelines in order to help you make the right choices for your school. However, differing perspectives from each diocese result in varying responses, which can make it difficult to establish a consensus opinion.

- Academy or not?
- Admissions under pressure
- Finding and appointing a new head teacher
- Appointing staff for a Catholic school

- Children and staff of other faiths in Catholic schools
- Chaplaincy provision and the shortage of priests today.

Academy or not?

Diversity of opinion is never more sharply focused than on the academy option. The question concerning whether to become an academy or not continues to vex both bishops and governors alike, with one point of view being that this is the best option for our children and may offer gains in premises, resourcing and expertise. However, the opposing view says there is a moral issue concerning the common good of all children, as well as a "grey area" concerning the present powers of the Secretary of State for Education, including the right to make radical changes to academy status without recourse to legislation.

The majority of dioceses have either left the decision up to the individual governing bodies or acted on their behalf, calling for all Catholic schools to become large multi-academy trusts. This has resulted in tension as just two dioceses, Liverpool and Salford, remain firm in their view that this is not the way forward in the present climate. However, if the government goalposts move, concerns may well change. Clearly, governors feel the weight of these challenging decisions and want to do what is best for their school. Weighing up the pros and cons is also difficult as this is such a new venture, and therefore the possibility of drawing on the experience of those who have become academies and examining the impact of this move over time is limited.

The challenge is in keeping the balance between the needs of a particular school's pupils and the bigger picture – the common good. Governors need to listen to all sides, and perhaps ask Chairs of governing bodies from other schools to come and share their experience in order to make an informed decision. Only time will tell the true worth and wisdom of academy status for the mission of the Church in education.

Admissions under pressure

The challenge of being able to predict what the demand for places in your school will be has become a complex issue. Demographic changes to the local area, wider catchment areas and sudden influxes of new arrivals continue to cause great concern for governors and families alike. Operating the admissions policy in a transparent and fair manner is essential. However, when you are in a position of being very oversubscribed this becomes increasingly challenging. Helping parents to understand this is also difficult because their number one concern is to get their child into your school. The majority of Catholic schools are high achieving and popular, much in demand and oversubscribed. Here the challenge to remain open to those who are in the greatest need can often be put to the test as schools consistently feel that they are under the microscope to ensure that they remain in top positions. Being and remaining a high-performing school means being so for all children. That is our mission. What it does not mean is using backdoor selection procedures, which not only break the law but also fail to comply with the Church's mission. Oversubscription also challenges the diocese and local parishes. The Church must provide for the education of Catholic children.

The sacred Synod earnestly exhorts the pastors of the church and all the faithful to spare no sacrifice in helping Catholic schools to become increasingly effective, especially in caring for the poor, for those who are without the help and affection of family and those who do not have the Faith.

Gravissimum Educationis, Declaration on Christian Education, 9

The Church as a mother is under an obligation, therefore, to provide for its children an education by virtue of which their whole lives may be inspired by the spirit of Christ.

Gravissimum Educationis, 3

The priority is clear. The means may be the real challenge, especially as we are called to "spare no sacrifice" in ensuring the education and formation of our children. When it comes to spelling this out in real terms, parents and teachers can sometimes feel very "let down" by the Church if the particular diocese does not support their request for expansion. Here it is a matter of demonstrating long-term basic need and demand. Expansion cannot be on the basis of one year's oversubscription, which is no comfort for those families who can't secure a place in your school. However, your head teacher can also help by talking to parents and encouraging those who are waiting for a place to remain on the waiting list because in many areas families move in and out regularly.

Finding and appointing a new head teacher

The news that your head teacher is moving on or retiring can be very unsettling for everyone because the head is the pivotal figure at every level within the school community and very important in the wider local community. However, it is also a moment of opportunity and growth. Good leaders know when they have fulfilled their part of the mission for the school and will move on. Some governors find this difficult to understand, as they often say, "But why go, when we are doing so well?" or "In my time the head was there for two decades, taught me and my children – you've only been here eight years!"

If the ongoing professional development of your head teacher is really effective you will encourage the head to develop to his or her full potential. It is often good for a head to seek a new challenge, recognising that this is what he or she needs. A primary head teacher of an infant school or a junior school may well feel the need to broaden his or her experience and look for a primary school covering all ages from Nursery through to Year 6. Or it may simply be that the head seeks a greater challenge in a different social environment. What is particularly impressive is when a head chooses to go to a school that is struggling, to bring it back to its full potential as an outstanding school.

At secondary level the reasons can be the same. Sometimes it can be because the head feels ready to go to a bigger school, or move into a more challenging or deprived area because of his or her commitment to those in the greatest need. To be honest there can be as many reasons as there are head teachers. What is important is to view the change as an opportunity for growth and development, however good your school is. There is always more to do because "outstanding" is where we should be; excellence is our lifelong goal!

So what do we do?

The appointment of the head teacher needs expert advice from the appropriate bodies. Many schools now engage HR (human resources) agencies, either from the local authority or from independent organisations. These can be and often are very helpful. However, before engaging any agency that is not part of the Catholic community it is really important to contact your diocese directly and ask for guidance and help. Current legislation is complex and requires a governing body to seek expert help. HR agencies do not operate within a Catholic framework and right from the first stages of the process governors need to be secure in the fact that they are following the correct procedures regarding the issues listed below, which all need to take into account the fact that there are particular requirements that are frequently not known by outside agencies – governors, too, sometimes!

- Advertisements
- Person specification
- Job description
- What should go in the pack to be sent to applicants?
- Selection processes including shortlisting and references
- Interviews
- Appointment
- Issue of CES contract
- Letting people know who the new head teacher is.

Naturally the head teacher must hand his or her resignation to the Chair of governors, in writing, before anything else can happen. Guidance for the appointment process is on most diocesan websites and very helpful information is also available by following the "Employment Documents" link at the Catholic Education Service website: **www.catholiceducation.org.uk/**

Key to getting it right is asking for advice from your Catholic Director of Education – he or she will actually be present or send an education officer or representative to be with you each step of the way from the initial discussions to the final appointment.

Know where you want your school to go

The process of finding and appointing a new head teacher is a weighty one for many governors. However, it is very important to discuss the following points as a full governing body. As a school, where are we now – what are our strengths and areas for development? Remember, this must be about your role as part of the mission of the Church in education. You must be the very best school you can be, a sign of hope and an example to your local community of what you stand for, which is nothing less than the transformation of society according to the values and beliefs of the Gospel and the teaching of the Church. It is a tall order and one that must come first in the selection of your new head teacher. Candidates may well have excellent qualifications and be able to answer in an impressive manner about headship and leading a school. But if they do not understand the mission of the Church and can't articulate what it is, then this is not the candidate for a Catholic school. The head is the role model for all.

You will be able to refer to your school development plan and hopefully each governor will have his or her own detailed specific knowledge of key areas. However, on this occasion this is not enough. Everyone needs to be clear about where they want the school to go in the next three to five years at least.

One simply has to ask:

- Are we all really confident that we know where we are now?
- Can each one articulate where he or she thinks the school needs to go?
- What is our common vision for the future?

What is not acceptable is simply to say, "Well, we just want to carry on the head's good work." Yes, carry on, but doing what and going where?

Having assisted a large number of governors in the process of selecting a new head teacher, I have always found that when governors come together to discuss their vision for the school as a Catholic learning community, for the present and the future, the process becomes much more focused. This shared vision then informs the selection process and the formulation of important questions.

Asking the big questions

Some governors find it difficult to formulate key questions about the Catholic life of the school, so the following are a few well-tried examples which might help. You will notice that they flow from your review and evaluation questions in Chapter 1 above, p. 16.

1. What would you consider to be the mission of the Church in education today?

2. How would you see yourself working with the governors in building up the Catholic life of the school as a centre of excellence and learning?

3. You have seen our mission statement – what is your response to it and how might you see yourself developing this in our school?

4. To what extent do you consider the learning in a Catholic school to differ from that in any other good or outstanding school?

5. Share with us how you see spiritual, moral, social and cultural education; and how would you know that it is actually being delivered?

6. How do you view the place of religious education in the curriculum and what do you consider its role to be?

7. Share with us how you see the role of continuing professional development in a Catholic school with reference to all staff.

8. The governors are keen to see leadership developed at all levels in the school. With particular reference to the building up of the Catholic life of the school, how would you go about this?

9. The governors are keen to develop leadership skills among our pupils so that they are able to take up their place in society as instruments of transformation. Share with us your thoughts and any ideas you have as to how you might go about this.

10. This school has a key role in building up the life of the Church both in the home and the parish. Share with us your thoughts and ideas about strengthening and developing these relationships further.

Appointing staff for a Catholic school

As governors we are challenged to try to appoint the best possible teachers who are also Catholic. We have discussed the necessity of the head teacher being a practising Catholic; the same requirement stands for the posts of deputy head teachers and people responsible for leading religious education. In areas where the Catholic population is sparse this is very difficult; governors can be tempted to follow the "three attempts" approach at getting a Catholic, and if they are not successful then going for a Christian of another denomination for these protected posts. Sadly, this only leads to an impossible position in which practising the Catholic life and witness to the faith is not possible for the leadership and those responsible for teaching the faith. While many good

practising Christians are great gifts to the school and are usually very supportive, they cannot witness in practice to that which they are not. This is the reason behind the bishops of England and Wales being so clear in this directive.

We are charged with persevering in our quest to find as many Catholic teachers as possible to teach in the school. When the number is limited, then the governors have a particular responsibility to see that all staff are helped to understand their role as educators in a Catholic school through an induction programme, training and formation in the mission of the Church in education. The companion publication to this book, *How to Survive Working in a Catholic School*, also published by Redemptorist Publications, may help in this process.

Naturally we have to be sensitive in how we do this; however, it is not acceptable to leave it to the newly arrived to just "pick it up".

Children and staff of other faiths in Catholic schools

This is nothing new. Catholic schools have long been culturally and socially diverse. The Catholic Education Service releases data from Ofsted each year which demonstrate the variances in makeup between Catholic schools and maintained schools that are not Catholic. In 2013–14 34.5% of pupils in maintained Catholic primary schools came from ethnic minority backgrounds whilst the figure for maintained schools nationally was 28.5%; and in Catholic maintained secondary schools 17.5% were from the most socially deprived areas whereas the national figure for other schools was 12.2%.

However, what is a rapidly changing picture in some areas is the increasing shift in population according to religious affiliation. We should not be too surprised at this. After all, are not the majority of Catholic families in this country able to tell a similar story? When many first arrived in the country, did they not look for where they could find a Catholic community, church, work and a place to stay? What we are seeing with other faith communities is a very similar story. As the newly arrived found a home, school and church, their children quickly acquired an education that enabled them to move upwards and out, only to be replaced by the next wave of newly arrived, who today are not always Catholic. However, the reputation of Catholic schools is renowned and much sought after by families of other faiths. Why? The reputation is one of high achievement, good discipline and values, and in the case of some faith groups they want to send their children to schools where faith comes first, even if it is not their faith. I remember being very moved at a school in Rochdale by a group of Muslim mothers who had deliberately moved their children from the local community school to the Catholic primary school. When I asked them why, one mother replied,

It is important for us that our children come to a school where they pray. We may be separated by religion but we are united in our spirituality. God is important in all our lives.

The Catholic Church recognises the importance of learning with and from all peoples of faith. The 1997 document *Catholic Schools and Other Faiths* from the Bishops' Conference of England and Wales has this to say: "all schools are being challenged by the reality of a multi-faith, multi-cultural society and by new developments in the Church's teaching".

The bishops recognise that "some Catholic schools – perhaps a small, but nevertheless significant group – are in the front line of change. These schools and the dioceses responsible for them need to consider with the support of the whole Catholic community how they should respond institutionally to the issues that arise."

One of the recommendations of this document specifically refers to the role of governors:

Formation of the Catholic Community

That the relationship between Catholics and people of other faiths be an area of formation and education for priests, teachers, and catechists and indeed for the Catholic community at large, so that the Catholic community can be informed partners in this work both at parish level, and in particular as parents of pupils in schools and also as Governors and prospective Governors.

The recommendations go on to further encourage governors to develop the spiritual formation of pupils of other faiths and "that governing bodies develop a process of dialogue and partnership with their local Other Faith communities".

Embracing children and families, as well as staff, of other faiths to be supported in their faith and its practice is very much part of the Catholic tradition.

The Catholicity of a school is not just defined by numbers of Catholics but by the strength of its commitment and faithfulness to the missionary thrust of the Church. As Pope Francis has reminded us, we are not just disciples of Jesus Christ, but must be "missionary disciples" living as a community for mission. This requires exceptionally strong leadership on behalf of the whole leadership team of the school, which of course includes the governors. Governors will find much to reflect upon in the document *Catholic Schools and Other Faiths*, which acts as a very valuable resource in dealing with the inevitable tensions that arise in multi-faith Catholic schools.[1]

Chaplaincy provision and the shortage of available priests today

The number of Catholic schools that are able to have regular visits by their priest is rapidly declining. As some dioceses reorganise parishes into clusters, with just one priest to minister to a group of parishes rather than the traditional model of each parish having at least one priest to serve it, we are now faced with a situation of fewer and fewer priests who have the time either to come into school regularly or to meet the growing chaplaincy needs within schools today. Many bishops have encouraged schools to appoint lay chaplains to work as part of the chaplaincy team. While this may seem a solution, it raises at least two big questions: Can the school afford to appoint this lay chaplain on a living wage? And, secondly, where are they going to get a suitably qualified and experienced trained lay chaplain? They do exist, but they are in short supply.

[1] See also Bishops' Conference of England and Wales, *Guidelines for the Study and Implementation of "Catholic Schools and Other Faiths"* (Chelmsford: Matthew James, 1997).

It was just this dilemma that was challenging the Diocese of Salford in 2011. The following is an outline of how the diocese responded to the chaplaincy needs of the schools who were without lay chaplains. The diocese are happy to share their experience with governors nationally. What they realised is that if the answer cannot be found outside the school then maybe a solution lies within. They asked themselves the questions:

"Who do we have within our community who could be trained for this ministry?"
In the first instance, governors looked to see if there were teachers who could take this on. But the problem was that teachers "taking it on" is not a solution when they are already working all the hours they can. It had to be new thinking! This is where they sought the advice of EducareM, an independent charity set up to support Catholic education nationally. It was at this point that the next question began to be explored:

"Is there a way in which the pupils themselves could be trained to help?"
One feature of a really good Catholic school is that the governors have an eye for spotting potential in the school community and then looking for new and challenging ways of helping this to grow and develop. You will be familiar with the many ways in which your school is developing leadership in the pupil body through a whole range of focus groups, buddies, prefects, school councils, eco councils, just to name a few. It seems the list gets longer every year! While these are all very important, what is not happening to the same degree is the development of leadership of young people for ministry within the Church. In days gone past this was often seen simply in terms of sending young people off to train for the priesthood or religious life. Thank goodness we have more sense now and leave such choices to the people themselves, and usually in later years. So the question broadened not just to look at the school but to ask ourselves how we can help young people to exercise leadership in the Church in an active and appropriate way. What transpired went far beyond what we anticipated and has had a very significant impact. We were going to "grow our own".

How did it all start?

The initial pilot of six primary schools began in the Diocese of Westminster, working with experienced head teachers and their parish priests.

We recognised that in every other area of school life we expect our pupils to "step up" and take on a considerable amount of responsibility. We entrust them with these responsibilities, recognising that they will carry them out. How often are we really surprised by the extent of their independence, maturity and willingness to give of their time and energy? So why not train them to be faith leaders?

Adult leader of the team – canonical restrictions

The definition of a lay chaplain is important because canonically the only person who can be called "chaplain" is an ordained priest appointed as such by the bishop. Therefore all other appointments are designated as "lay". Together they form the chaplaincy team.

As each new school takes up this model of chaplaincy it enters into a selection process that includes:

- The post of lay adult chaplain (not a teacher)
- Pupil chaplains (primary Y5, secondary Y10).

Who can apply?

Adults

Committed Catholic staff who have some experience as a catechist or background knowledge and experience. This post is best carried out by someone on the school staff who is already appointed in a supporting role rather than a full-time teacher. Applicants must be practising Catholics.

- Post is internally advertised
- Interview carried out by parish priest, governor, head and person responsible for RE.

Pupils

Pupils who are baptised Catholics and very committed to their faith, with good leadership skills and a confidence in relating to people across a wide spectrum. In the event that children who are not Catholic apply and are deemed to be ideal in every other respect, then the school is encouraged to contact the diocese for advice on how to proceed. Candidates then:

- Apply in writing
- Are shortlisted
- Undergo a professional interview conducted by the head, lay chaplain, parish priest and a governor

- Pupils make a five-minute presentation on "What I would bring to the chaplaincy of the school", followed by questions from the panel
- Are selected (eight for a primary school, maximum ten in a secondary school).

Once they have been selected, the diocese is informed and both the adult lay chaplain and the pupil chaplains attend a full day's training by the diocese, which comprises:

- Exploring their roles
- Creating the chaplaincy development plan
- Being appointed in the cathedral by the bishop's representative or in their parish by the parish priest
- Receiving their letter of appointment from the diocese or the parish priest.

Practice varies in each diocese; the greatest impact on the pupils, their families and the school is when the appointment comes from the bishop and is celebrated in the cathedral.

Monitoring and support
Ongoing support is provided by a visit to the school by the diocesan Department for Education and Formation as well as through EducareM.

Ongoing professional development for adult lay chaplains is provided by EducareM and the diocese in the form of:

- Training days
- Termly meetings
- Retreat days
- Extended certificated chaplaincy training programme.

Schools that are in their second year of the chaplaincy programme carry out the same appointment of pupil chaplains as before but it is done internally and in the parish. The parish priest informs the diocese of the names of those who have been selected. Their personal letters of appointment are then sent to the parish and presented at their commissioning celebration.

What difference is this making to our schools?
This is proving to be extremely successful. Pupils feel empowered. They are taking real leadership roles in the school. Being a member of the team is seen as the most important role for a pupil in the school. The team meet with the Senior Leadership Team and governors on a regular basis. Many schools have adjusted their uniform so that the pupil chaplains are easily identified, and they are provided with chaplaincy space in the school.

Pupils are leading through:

- Leading times of prayer and worship in classes
- Teaching and witnessing to their faith with younger children in the sacramental programme
- Running the media desk on a daily basis so that everyone knows what is going on
- Providing thoughts for the day/week
- Coordinating and encouraging charity work
- Reaching out to families and parishes in numerous ways.

An even greater challenge from head teachers in Salford

The story

The lay chaplaincy teams have been extremely successful with over one hundred schools now operating under this new model. It has been the selection process of pupil chaplains that has given rise to a growing concern about the way in which pupils who seriously wish to be part of the chaplaincy team may be excluded because either they are not baptised Catholics or they belong to another Christian denomination or faith group.

As an increasing number of heads enquired about what to do when they simply did not have enough Catholics to draw on to form the chaplaincy teams, we began a process of discernment about the way forward. Pivotal to this process were the following:

1. Our living out of the mission of the Church in education.

2. These are Catholic schools that must remain authentic and true to their core purpose.

3. What are these core purposes?

4. If a Catholic school admits pupils from other denominations and faiths, what are our reasons for doing this?

To help us in this process we went back to the following documents:

- *Code of Canon Law*
- Trust Deed
- Instrument of Government
- Ethos statement
- Teaching of the Church on Catholic education with particular reference to the models of Catholic schools found therein
- Teaching of the Catholic Church on inter-faith dialogue
- *Catholic Schools, Children of Other Faiths and Community Cohesion: Loving Tenderly, Acting Justly, Walking Humbly* (Catholic Education Service, 2008)
- *Meeting God in Friend and Stranger* (Catholic Bishops' Conference of England and Wales, 2010)
- *Catholic Schools and Other Faiths* (Catholic Bishops' Conference of England and Wales, 1997).

While there are many inspirational documents on inter-faith dialogue, the challenge was how to translate this into reality in a Catholic school in the Diocese of Salford.

With reference to the teaching of the Church on Catholic education over the past fifty years we recognised the following models as integral to the mission of the Church in education in the diocese.

Model 1 - A Catholic school where the majority of pupils and staff are all practising Catholics. This model is supporting those families for whom education and the practice of the faith are very important. It acts in support of the family and the parish in coping with all the tensions of the twenty-first century, bringing up their children as young people where life, faith and culture are integrated.

Model 2 - A Catholic school where the head teacher and senior leaders are Catholic but many of the pupils and staff may be either practising Catholics, from other faith traditions or no faith at all. Here the Church is responding to the need to support those who may not know Jesus Christ, struggle with many twenty-first century issues and in particular those who have been pushed to the fringes of society and become marginalised.

Model 3 - A Catholic school where there are very few Christians in the area, the head teacher and senior leaders are practising Catholics, but many others are not. Here the school is primarily acting as an agent of evangelisation, witnessing to Jesus Christ and the Gospel.

The context of schools in the Diocese of Salford

As far as the development of lay chaplaincy had been concerned we were clearly operating out of model 1. What we were being challenged to grapple with was the mission of the Church that is also found in models 2 and 3. We recognised that the majority of schools within the diocese were model 2 and a small number were closer to model 3 owing to the demographic changes in the population over the past fifteen to twenty years. Significant numbers of Hindu and Muslim families had relocated to particular areas, impacting on the local schools' intake. However, it is clearly the case that many schools are made up of pupils from a variety of religious backgrounds, even if the majority of pupils are Catholic.

Forcing the decision

The challenge became immediate on one occasion when a school on its way to the training day phoned to enquire, "Is it OK for our Muslim children to be commissioned today?"

Clearly this was a very difficult moment. Not wanting to embarrass or offend the school or make the Muslim pupils feel that they were not accepted, we had just one hour to find a way forward. As a result we took refuge in the 1988 Education Reform Act's requirement for every child to be spiritually, morally, socially and culturally educated, and at the end of the day the Muslim pupils were missioned to help develop the Spiritual, Moral, Social and Cultural education (SMSC) across the school. While this dealt with the immediate difficulty, it was neither satisfactory nor clear about the status of the team as a chaplaincy team. Nor did it really address the issue of the faith development of the pupils of other denominations or faiths.

The way forward

The questions were still with us:

- How do we enable pupils of other faiths and denominations to develop their faith?

- How can we be one united, authentic team?

- Is it chaplaincy or is it something else?
- So where does chaplaincy fit in?

In drilling down to what it was we were trying to do we recognised the following:

1. All pupils are admitted to a Catholic school because it is right for them to be there. The call to dialogue with other faiths and traditions is at the heart of the mission of the Church – engaging in a divine synergy which enables God in you to speak to God in me, taking us both to a place not yet discovered nor dreamed of.

In dialogue, Christians and others are invited to deepen their religious commitment, to respond with increasing sincerity to God's personal call and gracious self-gift, as our faith tells us, always passes through the mediation of Jesus Christ and the work of his Spirit.

Pontifical Council for Inter-religious Dialogue, *Dialogue and Proclamation* (1991), 40

2. All pupils are part of God's family.

First comes the fact that the whole of humankind forms one family, due to the common origin of all men and women, created by God in his own image.

Dialogue and Proclamation, 28

Since many of you do not belong to the Catholic Church and others are non-believers, from the bottom of my heart I give this silent blessing to each and every one of you, respecting the conscience of each one of you but knowing that each one of you is a child of God.

Pope Francis, Audience with journalists, 16 March 2013

3. All are called to live in communion.

Correspondingly, all are called to a common destiny, the fullness of life in God. Moreover, there is but one plan of salvation for humankind, with its centre in Jesus Christ, who in his incarnation "has united himself in a certain manner to every person"... Finally, there needs to be mentioned the active presence of the Holy Spirit in the religious life of the members of the other religious traditions. From all this the Pope concludes to a "mystery of unity" which was manifested clearly at Assisi, "in spite of the differences between religious professions."

Dialogue and Proclamation, 28

... this basic conviction in Vatican II is found in the Constitution Gaudium et Spes. *The Council teaches that Christ, the New Adam, through the mystery of his incarnation, death and resurrection, is at work in each human person to bring about interior renewal.*

Dialogue and Proclamation, 15

Let Christians, while witnessing to their own faith and way of life, acknowledge, preserve and encourage the spiritual and moral truths found among non-Christians, together with their social life and culture.

Nostra Aetate, Declaration on the Relation of the Church to Non-Christian Religions, 2

By admitting pupils of other faiths and traditions to the school the governors have the responsibility of developing or enabling the growth of every pupil's faith and their knowledge and understanding thereof. They are not there to "make up the numbers".

The G.I.F.T. model – "Growing in Faith Together"
An idea from Africa provided a way forward. The Rwandan people have a tradition that when they wish to give a gift of great value to someone they weave a grass basket and paint an intricate design on the outside. Every basket is unique and only given on a very special occasion. The basket is then presented to the person with the understanding that it contains the most precious gift that they have to give – their love, thanks, gratitude. Once given they should never be sold, as they contain the gift of great price. Religious communities and parishes often use them as tabernacles.

The governors agreed to take the next step
Two schools with a very high percentage of pupils of other faiths and denominations were invited to try this model. What happened was very moving. Parents, governors and head teachers all joined in the day of preparation and training at the diocesan centre. By focusing on the gift of faith that each one carried we were able to move forward in an authentic and honest way, recognising our diversity and difference while at the same time finding that which was common – the desire to know their God, and build up the community as it should be, a place of welcome, love and friendship to all our brothers and sisters as one family, one race – the human race.

Reflection

Do not be disheartened in the face of the difficulties that the educational challenge presents! Educating is not a profession but an attitude, a way of being; in order to educate it is necessary to step out of ourselves and be among young people, to accompany them in the stages of their growth and to set ourselves beside them.

Give them hope and optimism for their journey in the world. Teach them to see the beauty and goodness of creation and of man who always retains the Creator's hallmark. But above all with your life be witnesses of what you communicate. Educators... pass on knowledge and values with their words; but their words will have an incisive effect on children and young people if they are accompanied by their witness, their consistent way of life. Without consistency it is impossible to educate! You are all educators, there are no delegates in this field.

Thus collaboration in a spirit of unity and community among the various educators is essential and must be fostered and encouraged. School can and must be a catalyst, it must be a place of encounter and convergence of the entire educating community, with the sole objective of training and helping to develop mature people who are simple, competent and honest, who know how to love with fidelity, who can live life as a response to God's call, and their future profession as a service to society.

Pope Francis, Address to the students of the Jesuit schools of Italy and Albania, 7 June 2013

REFLECTION POINTS

- What is your response to this chapter? What has struck you?
- Of the issues highlighted in the chapter, which ones are currently challenging your school?
- How would you like to develop chaplaincy in your school?

CHAPTER 5

Review and self-evaluation: on message – on mission – on task

Wherever there may seem to be an opening for a new mission, we would prefer the erection of a school, so arranged as to serve temporarily for a chapel, to that of a church without one.

Westminster Provincial Synod, 17 July 1852

There is no lack of material from local authorities and governor support agencies offering help and advice as to how to go about a review and self-evaluation of governance. Therefore it is not my intention to reinvent the wheel. What it is important for us to consider is the context in which a governing body of a Catholic school sets about the process. Here help and materials for carrying out this process are patchy at best.

As governors we need to be very clear about what or who is in the driving seat. The barrage of emails and documents that fall into our in trays is never-ending and can feel quite overwhelming at times, particularly if the school is due an inspection. Understanding the river of communication is quite another matter. In this chapter we will focus on what it is we need to be keeping as our primary focus and benchmark while at the same time reviewing and evaluating our leadership. The task of review and self-evaluation, at its best, is an ongoing process, which serves to identify strengths and weaknesses of the governing body and raise the confidence of each member so that they are able to say:

- I understand the mission of the Church in education
- I know why I am here
- I understand my role
- I know what steps I need to take to develop in my role
- I feel confident in asking questions and seeking clarification
- I know where to go for help.

Equally important is the need to know your school at a deep level. Review and self-evaluation serves to provide the governing body with a true and honest picture of what is actually happening as opposed to what we think might be the case. Perception is often stronger than truth in influencing judgements.

Schools that have long enjoyed an excellent reputation can so easily slip into a coasting mode rather than looking creatively for the next steps in striving for excellence. Accurate, up-to-date information will then inform discussion and decisions about the way forward.

The challenge comes when, faced with so many demands on our time and expectations of our expertise, we can run the risk of simply going with what appears to be the biggest need at any moment. What we need to do is to say, "Wait a minute, this is interesting, important, but we must see how it fits with the mission of this school and set the latest requirement within that context." Or it might be important to say that this is not for us!

It is true to say that our role as governors has undergone a rapid change over the past few years as far as expectations from government are concerned. In 1996, the then Department for Education and Employment (DfEE) published *Guidance on Good Governance*, outlining what constituted good administrative practice. This was followed in 2000 by *Roles of Governing Bodies and Head Teachers*, clarifying how the roles of heads and governors should complement each other, with the governor's role being that of a "critical friend" to the school. You will find a breakdown of these distinctive areas on most diocesan websites under advice to governing bodies.

In 2003 a national training programme for new governors was launched focusing on the following three areas, which in turn needed to be put into an appropriate context for governors and leaders of Catholic schools:

1. Strategic role

The big picture as seen through – mission of the Church – transformation of society.

2. Critical friend

Asking the question, who, why, what, where, when and how, but supportive of the head teacher, recognising that they are the lead professional educator – governors offering ideas and engaging with the challenges facing the school – trust.

3. Ensuring accountability

At all levels in a spirit of stewardship and service – only the best is good enough.

The Ofsted *School Inspection Handbook* dated September 2014 calls for a much greater emphasis on the impact that governors are having on the leadership of their school. (See pages 40-51; however, be aware that this handbook frequently changes, so keep a regular eye on the Ofsted website [**www.ofsted.gov.uk/**] for the latest updates – big changes are being predicted in 2016.)

Inspection must examine the impact of leaders at all levels, including governors, and evaluate how efficiently and effectively the school is led and managed.

School Inspection Handbook, September 2014, p. 40

In reviewing and evaluating our effectiveness as a governing body the handbook outlines three core strategic functions:

a. Ensuring clarity of vision, ethos and strategic direction

So how are we living out the mission of the Church in education, as witnesses to Jesus Christ, educating and forming our young people to be "missionary disciples" for the transformation of society?

b. Holding the head teacher to account for the educational performance of the school and its pupils, and the performance management of staff

Ensuring that Canon 806 is our goal – "Those who are in charge of catholic schools are to ensure, under the supervision of the local Ordinary, that the formation given in them is, in its academic standards, at least as outstanding as that in other schools in the region."

c. Overseeing the financial performance of the school and making sure its money is well spent

Key consideration here for a Catholic school is the use of resources to support those pupils who are in the greatest need, which includes SEN and use of pupil premium.

In other words, what difference do we make to the effective running and delivery of education in this school and can we actually provide clear evidence of the impact of our governance? This is where some governors need help. During the diocesan inspection of schools carried out under Ofsted section 48 (diocesan schools have their inspections in two parts, section 5 carried out by an Ofsted team and section 48 carried out by diocesan inspectors appointed by the bishop) I have often come across head teachers who tell me theirs is a very supportive and effective governing body. However, when asked the question, "Can you tell me about the impact you feel your governing body has on the leadership of this school?" they sometimes find it very difficult to answer. It often takes quite a bit of digging to discover the true worth of their governance.

Where and how to start

A good place to start is with a reflective training session that looks at the whole governing body's understanding of the mission of their school today.

Reviewing and evaluating our effectiveness in the mission of the Church in education today

As a governing body, reflect together on each of the following questions. Invite each person to fill in his or her responses after a period of quiet reflection.

How informed are you as a governor about the mission of the Church in education?	
Has any training been offered to governors to help them access the Church's documents on education?	
What impact has this had on your understanding of your role?	
What is the mission for your school today?	
Do all governors agree on your priorities for mission?	
Is the mission statement known and understood by: Governors? How do you know?	

Teachers? How do you know?	
Children? How do you know?	
Parents? How do you know?	
Is the mission statement accessible to all pupils in the school? What makes you say this?	
Is your mission statement reflecting this? What evidence do you have to support your view?	
What evidence is there to show the impact of the mission statement on all aspects of school life?	
How often is the mission statement reviewed?	

A checklist of church documents on Catholic education can be found on pp. 13-14.

Knowing your school is critical to good decision-making and essential if we are going to be able to support the head teacher effectively and stay on mission.

We have looked at a review of how well we know the Church's mission in education and to what extent this is reflected in the mission of our school today. Now we need to turn to the important core purposes of a Catholic school. Here it is important to be very clear about what these core purposes are. Yes, exams, SATs and league tables are significant indicators of the effectiveness of the school's educational worth. However, these are all secondary to the "Why" of a Catholic school. Many of your neighbourhood schools will be good, some very good and some will be outstanding. Their key focus is the government agenda in education, which, sad to say, changes with each successive government. They are measured solely on how well this is being delivered. The core purpose for a Catholic school is much bigger and far more challenging. While we must deliver what we are required to do under the statutory obligations of the time our "Why" is very different, and in many cases so too is the "How".

You will recall from Chapter 1 that the Church has promoted the critical importance of Catholic schools because they are there for nothing less than the transformation of society. This is an enormous agenda and often leaves some governors feeling very inadequate. However, don't panic: the entire transformation is not expected to be completed on your watch!

Keeping things in perspective – quiet time of reflection

- Focus on a picture of a mountain blocking the route or way forward.
- Ask each person to reflect on how they might find the way forward even though it appears to be an enormous challenge.
- Play some quiet music as each one reflects on how this challenge might be overcome.
- Quietly in pairs share their thoughts.
- After a few minutes give each person a small square of sandpaper and ask them to discuss with their neighbour if this would help.
- After a few minutes pass a plate around with a piece of paper for each person with the words:

The power to shape the future is earned through persistence. No other quality is as essential to success. It is the sandpaper that breaks down all resistance and sweeps away obstacles. It is the ability to move mountains one grain at a time.

What is important is that we enable young people to continue the building of God's kingdom here on earth. In other words, making this world fit for all God's children.

Reviewing and evaluating the evidence for next steps

You may find this table helpful in assisting you to see how well equipped you and your governing body are to take your next steps. As governors, reflect together on the following questions. To what extent:

Are we being faithful to what the Church is calling us to do in educating young people to be able to challenge, change and transform the society in which they live? What evidence is there to support our views?	
Are we giving priority to those in the greatest need? What evidence is there to support our views?	
Is our school a place of hope, built on our belief that everyone carries a unique gift the world is waiting for? What evidence is there to support our views?	
Have we considered, and begun to include in our strategic planning, areas of development that address the above? What evidence is there to support our views?	
Are we engaging with the parish and local community so that we are seen as a place of welcome for all? What evidence is there to support our views?	
As a governing body, what are our next steps?	

The bishop through his diocesan advisers requires that every place of learning that carries the title "Catholic" be inspected by his appointed inspectors. Their task is to ensure that Catholic schools are authentically Catholic in all their dimensions. As we have discussed earlier, for the Catholic school nothing is secular. Every aspect of life within the school must be consistent with the core purpose, mission statement, aims and objectives of the school as a Catholic learning community.

As governors how do we know that this is the case?
We have already looked at our knowledge and understanding of the mission of the Church in education and also at evaluating our evidence in this regard. The bishop will ask for a detailed assessment, under the Ofsted section 48 inspection process, of key areas. What the inspectors will be evaluating is the effectiveness of the governors' role together with the head teacher and leadership team in ensuring that the school is actually delivering what it was set up to do. This encompasses the whole Catholic life of the school, the lived experience and witness of the community as a whole, as well as the academic learning. Dioceses vary in their approaches to the section 48 inspection process but all have the same common elements, of which they expect governors to have a clear knowledge and understanding. These are:

Leadership and management at all levels

Governors

What is the impact of their governance on all key areas of the life of the school? To what extent do governors witness to a Christ-centred learning community?

Head teacher

To what extent does he or she demonstrate a clear vision based on the teachings of the Gospel and the Church? Is he or she striving for excellence? Is he or she innovative, inspirational and clearly witness to a priority to those in the greatest need?

Senior and middle leaders

Are they confident in carrying out the mission of the Church in education, striving for excellence, empowered risk-takers who know how to translate the vision and mission of the school into their areas of responsibility?

Pupil leadership

Are they inspired and confident in taking on leadership roles which may be counter-cultural? Are they religiously literate and able to articulate the purpose and meaning of their learning as part of their development as people of challenge, change and transformation? Are they are striving to be the best they can be?

Overall effectiveness

Across the board how effective is the school in fulfilling its mission, aims and objectives – what is the impact on the pupils, local and wider community. Is the school a beacon of hope for all?

The school as a Catholic community

The school community

Does everyone (pupils, staff and families) feel valued and respected? How is this experienced at each level?

The wider community

How does the school impact on the local community and engage with the wider community nationally and globally?

Curriculum religious education

Attainment, achievement and progress in RE

Is it the lead area of attainment and achievement?

Quality of teaching

Are pupils receiving the best possible religious education, which is relevant, challenging and engaging with the big questions of the twenty-first century? Are they religiously literate?

Leadership and management of RE

Is it a leading example of excellence in the school? Are staff and pupils empowered and encouraged to be innovative, creative and take on responsibility for their own learning and faith development?

Pupils' spiritual, moral, social and cultural education and development

Are there clear links and connections made in all areas of learning and exploration, which ask the big questions of purpose and meaning, drawing on Catholic beliefs and values? Is this led as a key area, planned, well delivered, monitored and assessed? Do we as a governing body actually know what we are looking for?

Have a look at the following table and discuss together your understanding of each of these titles of education. Remember that SMSC education is the first entitlement of each pupil in the country, regardless of faith background. Every school must educate spiritually, morally, socially and culturally. This is not easy for schools that do not have a faith background as it is difficult to find the common core set of beliefs and values that inform our society and culture.

Table: Defining and evaluating SMSC education

Title Area	Definition	Evidence – Where and what to look for?
Spiritual	Signifies what we/I believe as Christians about the meaning and purpose of life, who we are, why we are here and where we are going. What is important is that all learning engages with the "big questions" across the curriculum. Key points: •Made in the image and likeness of God •Created in love and for love •All human beings are God's children •Each one is entrusted with a unique gift the world waits for •All human beings are God's children. Spiritual education engages with the big questions of purpose and meaning. It is everything about existence on this planet that is beyond the material.	Is there a governor who is linked to the development of SMSC education? Is there an appointed member of staff who has responsibility for developing SMSC education across the school? Do all staff understand what spiritual education is and how to deliver it? Is there appropriate and effective provision for in-service training for teaching and support staff? Is it planned into the teaching and learning for all pupils? Is there evidence of this planning, mapping? What is the impact of spiritual education on the pupils' learning and engagement with higher-order thinking and questioning across the curriculum? How is it monitored, assessed and evaluated? What supportive actions/decisions do governors need to make to develop this area further?
Moral	Because of what we believe about the purpose and meaning of life we live by principles and codes that guide our choices between right and wrong. Key points: •Because we are all uniquely made in the image and likeness of God this effects and influences our decisions •We cannot make any decision that contradicts or diminishes in any way the sacredness and importance of life •Our moral code impacts on our stewardship of the environment and the whole of creation.	Is there effective and regular in-service training provided for staff and governors to ensure professional confidence and competency in the delivery of moral education according to the moral teaching of the Church? Is it planned into the teaching and learning for all pupils? Is there evidence of this planning, mapping? What is the impact of moral education on the pupils' learning and engagement with moral issues across the curriculum? How is it monitored, assessed and evaluated? What supportive actions/decisions do governors need to make to develop this area further?

Title Area	Definition	Evidence – Where and what to look for?
Social	Because of our beliefs and values, our way of relating to self must be governed and informed by belief in the sacredness of life at all its stages. Key points: •Respect and care for myself •Respect and care for others •Ways of interacting socially. Must be influenced by our spirituality and our morality.	Is there effective and regular in-service training provided for staff and governors to ensure professional confidence and competency in the delivery of social education according to the spiritual and moral teaching of the Church? Is it planned into the teaching and learning for all pupils? Is there evidence of this planning, mapping? What is the impact of the school's social education on the pupils' learning and engagement with social issues across the curriculum? How is it monitored, assessed and evaluated? What supportive actions/decisions do governors need to make to develop this area further?
Cultural	The ways in which we do things – which develop over time within communities. Key points: •Rites •Rituals •Customs and practices. Culture gives expression to a community's spirituality, morality and social values. It is the way in which beliefs and values are celebrated and given expression.	Is there effective and regular in-service training provided for staff and governors to ensure professional confidence and competency in the delivery of Catholic cultural education according to the spiritual moral and social teaching of the Church? Is it planned into the teaching and learning for all pupils? Is there evidence of this planning, mapping? What is the impact of the school's social education on the pupils' learning and engagement with social issues across the curriculum? How is it monitored, assessed and evaluated? What supportive actions/decisions do governors need to make to develop this area further?

What needs to improve?

Finally the section 48 inspection will highlight key areas for development or improvement. This is very helpful as it gives the governors an objective view on how to go forward. Every school needs to know its next steps, whatever its inspection grade. The school must be a living, growing community always striving for excellence.

An innovative exception to the normal model

In 2013 the Diocese of Salford published a very interesting inspection schedule, *A Framework for Review, Evaluation and Celebration of our Catholic Schools in the Diocese of Salford*, which, although containing many of the same elements as other dioceses, has at the request of their head teachers pushed the concept of review and self-evaluation much further. Drawing on the work of Thomas Groome in his book *Educating for Life: A Spiritual Vision for Every Teacher and Parent* (Thomas More Press, 1998, pp. 203-212), the diocese categorised their areas for review, evaluation and celebration as what commonly became referred to as the five "W"s.

The diocese's Office for Education has taken each of these "W"s – Word, Welcome, Welfare, Worship and Witness – and interpreted them for Catholic schools across the diocese. To these they added Catholic Leadership, described in radical and challenging terms, which rests firmly on the model of Christ as servant.

The impact of this framework has been one of great challenge and, as one head remarked, "With this process there is no place to hide!" Governors have found it really helpful because of its rootedness in the Church's mission in education. Furthermore it is very clear that the section 48 inspection is no longer seen as just the RE inspection, which if one is really honest may not have been given the same rigorous attention by the leadership of the school as they would for the Ofsted section 5 inspection, which is led by an Ofsted-appointed team of inspectors. The Salford framework is so extensive that it is in fact more rigorous and demanding than the section 5 inspection. One might well argue that that is exactly what it should be, because it informs both the governors and the bishop as to the health of the school as a Catholic learning community, which must be the very best it can be. Nothing less is acceptable.

Governors, heads and teachers are provided with a very detailed analysis of what to look for in evaluating the effectiveness of each of the "W"s:

- Word
- Welcome
- Welfare
- Worship
- Witness.

This process provides a deep analysis of the area and clearly highlights both strengths and weaknesses. The framework invites the review and evaluation process to examine each area from the viewpoint of:

- The whole school
- The curriculum
- The pupils' experience.

As part of the ongoing governor training, governors are invited to attend training sessions on how to use the framework, not just for the purpose of preparing for Ofsted, but as a living, ongoing tool for review, self-evaluation and celebration. To involve as many governors as possible, some governing bodies have allocated each of the five "W"s to two or three governors to focus on for a year, assisted by a key member of staff. In this way it becomes manageable and governors and staff are engaged together in a constructive process of review and evaluation. It is important to have a standing item on the agenda of the governors' meetings to listen to the findings and progress of each team.

A full and comprehensive understanding of this innovative and very challenging framework can be found on the diocesan website: **www. dioceseofsalford.org.uk/**

Being "at home" in your school

Feeling part of the school community is not easy if you are not at least familiar with the premises and, most important of all, the people. One Chair of governors has created a simple checklist to see how well governors know their staff and the premises.

How well do you know our school?	
Have you met all the staff?	
Do you know your way around the school site?	
Are you familiar with the school day and class structure?	

Any other comments:
Please return this form to the Chair of governors

Having received the results of the survey, the Chair of governors then set about exploring ways of helping each governor become better acquainted with the school community. It was then a less daunting task for all governors to undertake the next, and more challenging, audit of their knowledge, skills and understanding

I am not sure I am skilled enough to be a governor today – it has all changed!

No one has all the answers or skills. That is why governors are drawn from a diverse variety of backgrounds. One complements the other. However, it is good to carry out a skills audit of each member of the governing body and see where each governor's real strengths lie. This helps in the formulation of the committees and also with working out whom to allocate for the oversight of the different areas of the school.

The following is a skills audit given to individual governors by the Chair of St Bernadette's Catholic Primary School in Kenton, Middlesex, so that they could invite governors to take a special responsibility in order to use their skills in the most appropriate place to ensure maximum effectiveness. You will notice that the third column is headed "Interest". In this way the Chair and governor responsible for governor professional development could see where members might like to be trained to engage more effectively in new areas.

St Bernadette's Governor Individual Skills Audit

How would you rate your knowledge, experience and interest on a scale of 1-5, where 1 = little or none, and 5 = extensive?

Areas of expertise	Knowledge	Experience	Interest
Strategic planning			
Vision and mission of St Bernadette's			
Marketing			
Project management			
Presentations			
Research			
Training			
Team-working			
Legal knowledge			
Chairing meetings			
Clerking meetings			
Administration			
Awareness of information/sources			
SIP			
SEF (48 and 5)			

Areas of expertise	Knowledge	Experience	Interest
School profile			
Strengths and weaknesses of the school			
Short- and long-term school priorities			
The Ofsted inspection process sections 48 and 5			
Curriculum			
SMSC			
RE			
Early Years/ Foundation			
Infants (KS1)			
Juniors (KS2)			
Maths/ Numeracy			
English/Literacy			
Science			

Name: ______________________

Date completed: ______________________

Areas of expertise	Knowledge	Experience	Interest
PE/Sport			
Art/Design/ Creative Curriculum			
ICT			
PSHE			
Languages (please state)			
Extra-curricular activities			
Extended schools services			
Special Educational Needs			
Premises			
School building and maintenance			
Health and safety			
Contracting services			
Premises management			

Areas of expertise	Knowledge	Experience	Interest
People			
Well-being (Staff)			
Public relations			
Communication			
Listening			
Mediating			
Personnel management			
Recruiting/ interviewing			
Equal opportunities			
Performance management			
CPD			
Finance			
Financial planning			
School financial management			
Best value			

Relevant experience

Please give further details of any work-related/personal experience you can bring to this governing body.

Training

Have you undertaken the governor induction course? (please circle) Yes/No
Was it: Diocese/LEA?
Please give brief details of courses you have undertaken in the past three years – include governor training and/or work-based training

Other training

Would you like more information on a particular topic, or is there a particular subject you would like training on?

Some creative ways of getting to know your school

Governor open days

Governors are invited to sign up to observe the activities that the pupils are engaged with throughout the day.

Advice: Try to get a range of experiences both in the classroom and outside it. Remember it is the child's experience that you are really trying to find out about most of all.

Back to school for the day

Here the governors are given a "buddy" and actually join the class for the day to experience what it is like. They do everything that the children do, without any exceptions! This is a great way of really learning about your school from the pupil's perspective.

Advice: Select a year group that you know the least about so that you can gain as much as possible from the experience. The children will be delighted to help you, so ask as many questions as you need. Remember, live their day with them – do as they do.

Work experience day

In this activity the governor is adopted for the day by a member of the support staff and again sees the day from their perspective, doing as much with the member of staff as it is appropriate to do.

Advice: Choose an area that you know little about so that you really see the extent of their responsibilities, challenges and areas where they really excel. Arrive and depart together.

Head teacher for a day

This can be one of the most eye-opening fact-finding experiences. Without altering anything of the head's day, join the head from the moment of arrival until he or she departs in the evening!

Advice: Get a good night's sleep before you undertake this activity. It may well be a very long day!

An invitation to tea

A small group of governors invites a cross section of children from a key stage to afternoon tea in school. Make it really special: cups and saucers, sandwiches and cakes, the full works. During tea ask the children to talk about their school. What they enjoy, really like – and what they would like to change.

Advice: Choose a special setting so that this really is an occasion. Keep the children in a key stage so that the range is not too great and the younger ones don't get left behind. Keep your questions open-ended so that you let the children respond as fully as possible in their own way. Six to eight pupils are enough.

Getting the right support for your role

Your first port of call is naturally your diocesan website, where hopefully you will find advice and support on a whole range of topics. However, these sites vary in content and quality. The availability of materials for a review and self-evaluation process of a governing body within the Catholic context are, as I said above, limited.

A further Catholic source for governors is the Catholic Education Service (CES) website: **www.catholiceducation.org.uk**

Some useful sites for resources, which are not Catholic but could be contextualised

The Department for Education's *Governors' Handbook: For governors in maintained schools, academies and free schools*, dated September 2014, is helpful and available in school. Have a look at paragraph 1.7.3, which has very helpful advice on governors' self-evaluation as a preparation for an Ofsted inspection. Click on the highlighted "Twenty key questions for a school governing body to ask itself". However, remember the Catholic context questions and make this information part of your review.

The **National Governors' Association** is a registered charity that offers a wide range of support and advice to governors and is easily accessible at **www.nga.org.uk/**

They offer guidance and resources for governors' review and self-evaluation as well as an external review service with an outside assessor.

GLM (standing for Governance, Leadership and Management) is the name of the organisation managing "Governor Mark", working with partners to promote and support the National Standards and Governor Mark process and can be found at **www.glmpartnership.org/index.html**

This is a very helpful form of external evaluation of the quality of governance in a school, providing a very thorough health check. More and more governing bodies are now using this process. If you are not familiar with it, it would be well worth the whole governing body having a look at the Governor Mark Standards Document at **www.glmpartnership.org/governor_mark.html**

By undertaking this process you will be able to demonstrate how you are impacting on school improvement, pupil outcomes, and evidence of supporting and challenging the school as well as your shared strategic leadership.

Governor induction: with every new governor the governing body changes

The effectiveness of the whole governing body is dependent on the ability of each member being able to contribute in the best way possible. The first few meetings can be very daunting, which is why it is important that governors feel safe and able to operate out of their strengths. The induction of new governors varies greatly, but is an essential part of quickly being able to become effective.

The Ofsted *Governors' Handbook* is an important guide for all governors. However, it is generic and, although helpful, won't help with all the particular characteristics of your school.

Every governing body should have someone responsible for governor induction. Many schools do. However, if as part of your review and self-evaluation process you discover that you don't have someone responsible for governor induction, then this needs to be addressed quickly.

A DIY response: St Augustine's Catholic High School, Clitheroe

The origin of the Governor Induction Pack dates back to the time when I was elected as a parent governor at a State school; where despite being enthusiastic and well intentioned, I found myself floundering, confused and overawed by the level of responsibility I was taking on and the role I was expected to play.

As a newcomer, I naively expected to be helped, if not spoon-fed – with a ready selection of "how to" guides, or failing that a guardian angel to guide me through the process of filling in the gaps. This was not to be! Far from being spoon-fed, I realised early on that I was facing starvation rations, with the meagre diet of "help" on offer. While my colleagues on the governing body were well meaning and did their best to point me towards publicly available information, I personally found the usual prescribed sources of help to be somewhat mechanical, anodyne and detached from my experience as a new governor.

When I was asked to join St Augustine's governing body as a foundation governor, I was again overawed – but this time for a different reason. I was humbled to be asked to join what was an already outstanding body of governors. Having finally accepted, it was my resolve to continue developing myself – but more importantly to ensure that any new governor that we recruited would not have to endure the lengthy apprenticeship that I had served. It furthered my conviction that from the outset governors should be clear about their purpose and equipped with the knowledge and skills to ensure clear, strategic direction, promote the ethos and values of our community – in order ultimately to deliver the high standards and outcomes for our children. In short, new governors should be able to join the body and "hit the ground running". It was my intention to demystify the role of governor without trivialising it, and to provide an "at a glance" guide without skirting round issues. The Induction Pack was born.

By devising our own bespoke guide based around the characteristics of our school, a dual purpose was served; not only were governors able to learn the ropes quickly, but it also helped to promote and safeguard our Catholicity. It does not claim, however, to have transformative properties, to be the fount of all knowledge, nor does it hold all the answers – it continues to be a work in progress. But when it is used – and this is the key – in conjunction with a mentor, this in theory should enable the words to be brought to life in a meaningful way, as the mentor metaphorically handholds the new recruit through the induction process.

As governors of a Roman Catholic high school, we are so much more than a set of skills or "competencies", as our HR brethren would say. Being a governor takes a lot more than having a passing interest or just commitment alone. The simple purpose of a customised Induction Pack is to harness and maximise the personal and unique attributes that characterise each and every one of us, as it simply allows us to get on with the job in our own special way and to add our part to the greater whole.

It is an exercise in commitment and faith towards a common goal, providing our children with the education they deserve, and fulfilling the Church's mission to form and educate our young people to be builders of a society fit for the next generation – perhaps best summed up by our School motto: Fides-Heredes – "Inheritors of the Faith".

Caroline Muldoon, governor responsible for induction

Comments from governors

When I was elected as a teacher governor, the Induction Pack was really useful. It gave me a clear picture of my roles and responsibilities and allowed me to feel part of the team from the first meeting.

Matt Haworth, teacher governor

The Induction Pack was very comprehensive in terms of factual content, and not only did it give me a clear idea of what was expected, but Mrs Muldoon was able to take me through it and bring to life some of the more specific advice, making it meaningful in the context of St Augustine's governing body, and in particular our Roman Catholic ethos.

Peter Livesey, parent governor

Over time St Augustine's have responded to the changing needs of governors and developed a comprehensive programme, which they are happy to share and advise schools on. The contents list below gives an overview of the extent of the induction process.

INDUCTION PACK CONTENTS

Introduction

Governors' Schedule/Terms of Reference

School Mission Statement

St Augustine's Governors' Prayer

St Augustine's Prospectus

Roles and Responsibilities of School Governors

Instrument of Government: Voluntary Aided School

Trust Deed from Diocese of Salford

Foundation Governors' Handbook

Governing Body Code of Practice (Diocese of Salford)

Model Code of Practice for School Governing Bodies (LCC)

Governors' Statutory Responsibilities

Model Policy for Governors Visiting

Visit Report Template

Recommended Journals

Governing Bodies and Effective Schools

Research on the Role of School Governors

Further Information

Governor's E-Learning (GEL) (includes sample copy)

Mentor Contact Details

Don't reinvent the wheel – St Augustine's ready to help!

Contact your diocesan education office and ask them for advice on which schools have a good induction process and documentation. This will help you to get started on compiling your own. St Augustine's are very happy for you to use their ideas or contact them for advice; for contact details see the school's website: **www.sarchs.com/**

Early warning signs

All schools go through difficult times and for some this can be prolonged. However, when you begin to have concerns, **don't wait**! This is the moment to share your observations with the Chair in confidence. In this way you may discover that it has been noticed by others and support is in place. However, it may be the case that you are the first to raise it. Putting it on the back burner is not the answer; neither is rushing in with guns blazing. Again, if this is something that the Chair is not sure how to proceed with, then the Chair must seek help quickly. It may just need a telephone conversation with the diocese or support services to advise the appropriate way forward. Leadership is always proactive, calm, but clear.

Support for the head teacher in difficult times is critical. Heads are human too! A good governing body will keep a close eye on work/life balance and well-being. The following is a short list of ways in which governors can help the head to keep a good work/life balance:

- A short retreat once a year financed by the governors' fund.
- Ensuring the head has a spiritual director/guide.
- Encouraging the head to work from home when he or she is working on demanding tasks such as the development plan, bids, reports etc.
- Time away from school to think, envision, develop new ideas.

All of these tasks are impossible from a head's office. Investing in quality time and provision for the well-being of your head will make a significant difference to the head's leadership, relationships and the way in which he or she can advise and guide the governors.

Watch your time too!

The endless round of meetings that heads and governors need to attend often run way over time, causing everyone to become frustrated and worn out. A policy of firm timekeeping may seem overly controlling, but everyone will thank you for it in the end. Meetings that go on over ninety minutes to two or three hours quickly degenerate into endurance mode and people switch off. It is far more productive to use a well-organised committee system with minutes sent out in advance outlining actions to be taken at the full governors' meeting than everyone talk through every topic on a mammoth agenda. One governing body I know well has a wonderful mechanism for keeping everyone to time. They have empowered the clerk to stop people from "going on" by presenting the clerk with a bell. Agenda items are timed (within reason!) and as soon as the time is reached the clerk rings the bell and says, "We have reached the time limit, how would you like to proceed?" Usually there is a resounding "Move on!"

The importance of celebration

I have always found governors very keen to offer support at all times but also when appropriate not to miss any opportunity to celebrate achievement and success. This does not have to be a major event, but small, real moments to recognise a job well done, a room that is a place of joy and excellence for learning, a teacher or member of staff who has gone beyond the call of duty. One can never underestimate the card or letter from the governors that shows recognition and thanks to a member of staff or pupils.

Reflection

The hero is one who kindles a great light in the world, who sets up blazing torches in the dark streets of life for men to see by. The saint is the man who walks through the dark paths of the world, himself a light.

Felix Adler

Nothing is so strong as gentleness. Nothing is so gentle as real strength.

St Francis de Sales

Every man, every woman who has to take up the service of government, must ask themselves two questions: "Do I love my people in order to serve them better? Am I humble and do I listen to everybody, to diverse opinions in order to choose the best path?" If you don't ask those questions, your governance will not be good.

Pope Francis

REFLECTION POINTS

- How much time is given to reflecting on why you are a governor?
- Has your governing body carried out a skills audit in order to inform their strengths and areas for development?
- If the audit has been carried out, is everyone clear about what needs to be done and are these steps being taken?
- Do you have a programme for inducting new governors? Is it carried out?
- How do you think you could get to know your school at a deeper level?

CHAPTER 6

What is expected of governors when Ofsted calls?

Good leaders are aware of both their strengths and weaknesses. They are not afraid to admit to the latter. They know how to find support and are humble enough to ask for it. There is no perfect leader who has all the gifts necessary for good leadership.

Jean Vanier [1]

Governors usually want only the best for their schools and it is when they know that the school is due to be inspected that even the most experienced can sometimes feel a little vulnerable. The constant pressure to keep abreast of the numerous changes in education is not easy to manage even for the most experienced governors.

Our head teacher has just reminded us that we are due for an Ofsted inspection in this academic year. When our school was last inspected we did very well overall in both sections 5 and 48. I have been part of many inspections and it has been a real privilege for me to serve as a governor across all phases for the past forty years. Not all in the same school, of course!

Over the years I have been a foundation governor, vice chair and now Chair of my present school in North London. My interest is also my passion to support Catholic education wherever I can. I know how critical governors are to a school and particularly for the head teacher. The pace of change in education today is at such a rate that even long-serving, experienced governors can sometimes feel at sea about what they need to do. As Chair of governors I need to constantly keep myself updated but also help all the board members feel secure in their governance.

[1] Jean Vanier, *Community and Growth* (Mahwah, NJ: Paulist Press, 1989), pp. 220-21.

I find governors are generous and willing, but it is very important for us to understand our role and responsibilities as employers representing the bishop. At all times we must act with integrity and discernment, recognising that the head and staff are the professionals. However, the governors have a duty to make themselves aware and familiar with all school matters. Even with all our experience on the governing body we feel the need to really understand what is expected of us. I try to keep up to date to help my governing body to know what is going on. However, I sometimes worry that I may be missing something important.

Pam Singh

Don't panic, this chapter will try to help you to focus on the key areas governors need to be confident about for both sections 5 and 48. Remember, the head teacher will help you – just keep asking the questions you want answered. Have a look at the Ofsted website, where you will see that Ofsted has drastically slimmed down its guidance by 275 pages as of September 2014! There are now just three guidance documents:

The framework for school inspection; the School inspection handbook; and Inspecting safeguarding in maintained schools and academies.

Key changes

- *The revised School inspection handbook incorporates guidance and briefings for inspectors that were previously spread across a number of documents. The exception is in the area of inspecting safeguarding, where guidance is set out in a separate document.*
- *While there is no fundamental change to inspection methodology, inspectors will from September 2014:*

- make graded judgements for early years and sixth form provision, following our consultation earlier this year;

- no longer record on evidence forms a grade on the quality of teaching for individual lesson observations;

- pay even greater attention to a school's curriculum to ensure that it is appropriately broad and balanced to help prepare young people for life in modern Britain.

- *Guidance has also been revised to support inspectors in making judgements following the phased removal of National Curriculum levels from September 2014.*
- *Schools previously judged to be good will no longer receive an interim assessment letter in the third year after their last section 5 inspection to inform them that they will not be inspected in the forthcoming year. Our inspection selection policy for "good" schools remains unchanged.*
- *The inspection handbook makes clear that the most important role of teaching is to promote learning and the acquisition of knowledge by pupils and to raise achievement. It reiterates Ofsted's stated policy that we have no preferred teaching style; it is up to the classroom teacher to determine how they should teach.*
- *There is clear guidance for inspectors on the duties and responsibilities of school governors.*[2]

2 Accessed at: www.ofsted.gov.uk/news/revised-guidance-for-inspections-of-maintained-schools-and-academies

Schools usually have a fair idea of the term in which they may be inspected, as long as the school was found to be good or better at the last inspection. (If a school falls below good, then the visits are more frequent and follow a different timescale, and are inspected under what is known as a section 8 inspection. This is quite a different format and process.) The precise date for the Ofsted section 5 inspection is not known until the phone rings at midday on the day before the Ofsted team's arrival. Or, in the worst-case scenario, it is fifteen minutes before they appear at the front door! In most dioceses there are at least two working days' notice before the Section 48 inspection, and in many it is longer. The imminence of an Ofsted inspection can sometimes weigh very heavily on the leadership of a school. However, head teachers are generally well clued up on what is expected of them, their governors, staff, pupils and families.

Preparing for Ofsted section 5 inspections

The really steep learning curve has been for the governors. As each new edition of the Ofsted *School Inspection Handbook* is published we have seen the governors' role become more prominent, with greater accountability for the leadership and management of the school. The latest edition of the Ofsted handbook (which came into effect on 14 September 2014) has gone even further.

If you have not already seen this document make sure that it has not been superseded as they tend to change frequently, and we know that by the end of 2015 there will be further quite significant changes to the way in which Ofsted approaches the whole inspection process.

On 9 October 2014 Ofsted's Chief Inspector for Schools, Sir Michael Wilshaw, stated that:

It is absolutely vital that this progress is sustained and that our system does not falter. Over two-thirds of good schools and colleges maintain their performance, and so there is a strong case for more proportionate inspections which focus on a professional dialogue between head teachers and inspectors.[3]

This promises to be a major shift in emphasis and one that governors and leadership teams would welcome. Sir Michael Wilshaw went on to outline the areas of focus for the new common inspection framework,

I believe that our new inspections should place emphasis on safeguarding, the breadth of the curriculum in schools, the relevance of courses and training in further education and skills, and the quality of early learning. Only then will we be able to make sure that all children and learners are properly safeguarded and prepared for life in the modern world.

The consultation also sets out proposals for four categories of judgements:

- *Leadership and management*
- *Teaching, learning and assessment*
- *Personal development, behaviour and welfare*
- *Outcomes for children and learners.*

[3] Accessed at: https://www.gov.uk/government/news/consultation-on-radical-changes-to-inspection

Whatever the changes and regardless of whether you are due an inspection or not, it would be well worth your time having a look. Naturally the moment you begin to read through this weighty document many questions arise. Don't worry – they do for everyone, depending on your background in education. Just because you're a teacher or even a head teacher does not mean that what is required is all that clear.

As I mentioned in the previous chapter, there is a good deal of help available for governors in understanding their role and the latest inspection requirements. However, if you are in an area where there is little local help, your head teacher is the first port of call. He or she will have had the latest training and have a pretty good grasp of the inspection process.

In the rest of this chapter I will outline the key responsibilities that the handbook identifies and offer some help as to what you may need to do and where you can find the answers.

So what is an Ofsted section 5 inspection?

Many governors ask what Ofsted stands for and who they are. Ofsted stands for: "Office for Standards in Education, Children's Services and Skills".

So what is it set up to do?

Simply put, it is the government's education health check on your school, but it also goes further, with a wide and far-reaching brief:

Ofsted regulates and inspects childcare and children's social care, and inspects the Children and Family Court Advisory and Support Service (Cafcass), schools, colleges, initial teacher training, further education and skills, adult and community learning, and education and training in prisons and other secure establishments. It assesses council children's services, and inspects services for looked after children, safeguarding and child protection.

Ofsted inspects and regulates to achieve excellence in the care of children and young people, and in education and skills for learners of all ages.[4]

So what is a section 48 inspection?

This is an inspection carried out in the name of the bishop as the person legally responsible for Catholic schools in the diocese, to ensure that your school is fulfilling its responsibilities to provide the best possible Catholic education for every pupil. For the Catholic community the section 48 inspection is the most important part of the inspection process.

The canonical and statutory requirements for inspection by the bishop

The bishop is the "first teacher" in the diocese with responsibility for the formation and education of his people, with particular responsibilities in all Catholic schools for children and young people from the early years foundation stage to sixth form.

4 Accessed at: www.ofsted.gov.uk/sites/default/files/documents/about-ofsted/s/Supporting%20narrative%20to%20the%20publication%20of%20Ofsted%20organograms%20and%20senior%20salaries%20information.pdf

Canon 804 §1

The formation and education in the catholic religion provided in any school… is subject to the authority of the Church.

Canon 803 §3

No school, even if it is in fact catholic, may bear the title "catholic school" except by the consent of the competent ecclesiastical authority.

Canon 806 §1

The diocesan Bishop has the right to watch over and inspect the catholic schools situated in his territory, even those established or directed by members of religious institutes.

As we have already mentioned in Chapter 1, the bishop delegates many of his responsibilities to the governors; that is why you will read in the Ofsted *School Inspection Handbook*:[5]

The inspectors who conduct **section 48 inspections** *are appointed by the school's governing body, or the foundation governors in a foundation school, having consulted with persons prescribed in regulations (normally the appropriate religious authority). The inspectors are normally drawn from the relevant faith group's section 48 inspection service, although not all faiths have their own inspectors organised in this way. Section 48 inspections should be approximately every five years. (p. 8)*

All dioceses have their own inspection service and arrangements. Your head teacher will notify the diocese as soon as possible once he or she knows that a section 5 inspection is about to take place. However, this does not necessarily trigger a section 48 inspection. In 2014 these two inspections were "uncoupled", leaving the bishop free to carry out the section 48 inspection according to the required timescale:

If a school (including an academy) is designated as having a denominational religious character, then denominational religious education, school ethos and the content of collective worship are inspected under section 48 of the Education Act 2005. (p. 8)

It is important to be aware that the section 5 lead inspector will check with the governors that arrangements have been made for a section 48 inspection within the correct time frame according to your previous grading from the last inspection. (See *School Inspection Handbook*, September 2014, p. 9.)

Do the section 5 Ofsted inspectors inspect RE?

This is a very important question. Yes, they can observe an RE lesson but with clear boundaries. (See Ofsted *School Inspection Handbook* – again, check you have the latest version.)

[5] Quotes throughout the rest of this chapter, unless otherwise stated, are from the September 2014 edition of the Ofsted *School Inspection Handbook*

In schools with a religious character, section 5 inspectors may comment on educational issues such as the contribution of assemblies to pupils' personal and spiritual, moral, social and cultural development, or the quality of teaching in any subjects, including religious education (RE). (p. 8)

This is not an easy path to tread. Making a judgement about teaching and learning without making reference to the content would be very challenging. However, the head teacher will ensure that the line is not crossed. It would be well worth discussing with your head teacher whether or not the head feels that he or she should accompany an inspector in any observation of RE.

So why two inspections?

Actually it is really only one inspection in two parts. The terms "section 5" and "section 48" refer to two sections of the Education Act of 2005 where the Ordinary (the bishop) is recognised as the rightful authority. This all links back to the 1944 Education Act, which established Catholic schools within the state-maintained sector on the grounds that as a minority group we had the right to educate our children according to our own beliefs, values and traditions as a Catholic community. In practice it does feel like two inspections.

What should governors do to be prepared for a section 5 inspection?

As we said in Chapter 5, the key is to know as much as possible about your school. A section 5 inspection will focus on:

- Quality of leadership and management
- The behaviour and safety of pupils at the school
- Quality of teaching in the school
- Achievement of pupils at the school
- The effectiveness of early years provision: the quality and standards
- Effectiveness of sixth form provision: the quality of education provided in the post-sixteen study programmes
- Evaluating the quality of boarding and residential provision in schools.

So let's look at the main areas, remembering that this is not a checklist but a means to helping your governors to know and understand their school at a deeper level. At every stage we need to be asking, "What is the impact of our decisions and actions on the life of the school as we strive for excellence in all areas?" You will recall from Chapter 1 that long before any government thought of Ofsted, the Catholic Church had already set the bar very high, saying that Catholic schools must be at least outstanding in all aspects:

Canon 806 §2

Those who are in charge of catholic schools are to ensure, under the supervision of the local Ordinary, that the formation given in them is, in its academic standards, at least as outstanding as that in other schools in the region.

Quality of leadership in and management of the school

Inspection must examine the impact of leaders at all levels, including governors, and evaluate how efficiently and effectively the school is led and managed. (p. 40)

We need to be able to demonstrate how the strategic decision-making and implementation instigated by the governing body have made a real difference to the learning and life of the school from early years through to the sixth form, where applicable. This is not easy to identify, which is why it is so important that the minutes of governors' meetings really do record accurately the decisions that have been made and then at subsequent meetings show evidence of monitoring and follow-up demonstrating the impact of the actions. A close reading of the Grade descriptors for leadership are uncompromising in their language as they refer to the need to engage in:

The pursuit of excellence in all of the school's activities. (p. 49)

This is to be evidenced through:

an uncompromising and highly successful drive to strongly improve, or maintain, the highest levels of achievement and personal development for all pupils over a sustained period of time. (p. 49)

Governors of Catholic schools must desire only the very best for their pupils, especially those in the greatest need, therefore:

All leaders and managers, including those responsible for governance, are highly ambitious for the pupils and lead by example. They base their actions on a deep and accurate understanding of the school's performance and of staff and pupils' skills and attributes. (p. 49)

Data are not always easy to grasp, particularly if they are not about your field of expertise. However a simple question to the head such as, "Please can you explain this chart, or these statistics, to me?" may help, rather than keeping quiet and hoping someone else around the table can grasp what it is all about or what the data tell us about pupil progress. Once you have a working knowledge of the data then don't stop asking questions! The head will be delighted that you are trying to understand. We are charged with the pursuit of excellence, not because Ofsted demands it but because this is what our children deserve. Ofsted will be looking at just how we are doing this.

Inspectors should consider how well leaders, managers and governors pursue excellence, modelling professional standards in all of their work. (p. 40)

Remember this is not just academic excellence but also relationships, behaviour, respect within a culture of high expectations and aspirations in all things. They will be looking at how the adults in the school model these high professional standards and aspirations.

It is not easy to get the balance right between affirming and supporting the head teacher and his or her team and applying the appropriate challenge as a critical friend:

Governors, or those with a similar responsibility, stringently hold senior leaders to account for all aspects of the school's performance. (p. 49)

Celebrating the strengths and achievements of your head teacher

Inspectors should pay particular attention to the contribution being made by the headteacher and ensure that they give sufficient credit where a head teacher is bringing about improvement in the school. (p. 40)

Don't leave it to the inspectors to articulate and celebrate the achievements and strengths of your head teacher. It is really important that all governors can identify exactly what the head teacher has done to improve the education and life of the school community and outline the achievements with specific evidence. It is not enough to keep saying, "We have a very good head teacher," because the inspectors will respond, "How do you know?" Perception and truth may not always be the same. Remember, examination or SATs results alone are not enough.

As a governing body it is important to be able to show that you are striving for excellence for every pupil and person in your school. Ofsted's criteria are high but the Catholic community's are much higher. They are only fully achieved in heaven! I always smile at the pre-section 48 phone call with some head teachers who begin the conversation with the comment, "You are most welcome, Sister. We are an outstanding school." I am tempted to reply, "As you should be!"

Supporting your head teacher is critical to the success of the school. A head teacher in conflict with the governors cannot lead effectively; neither can the governors carry out their leadership role in a constructive and helpful manner. When the governors are clear and unequivocal about the strengths of the head teacher and can articulate why and how the head teacher has made a significant contribution to the ongoing development of the school, giving clear examples and evidence to back up their judgements, then we are clearly operating at an effective level.

Your head teacher may well be supporting another school to develop, or you may be part of a federation, chain or group of schools:

with an overarching board and chief executive officer that assume some of the responsibilities formerly shouldered by the individual school governing body. (p. 40)

If this is the case then:

... inspectors should seek evidence of the impact of the overarching board and its staff as well as the school's local board, committee or governing body. (p. 40)

What the inspectors will be examining is the impact of these infrastructures and if the use of the resources to support them is actually good value for money and having the best possible impact. Again they are looking at the decisions and actions of the governors at all levels to see if they really do know and understand the implications of these more complex arrangements for governance. This will also extend to schools who are managing children's centres.

Vision, energy and growth

Fear should never be the driving force for any group or community. What unites and energises a school community is vision. In the words of St Paul, we are striving to be transformed in love and through love:

But strive for the higher gifts... If I speak in the tongues of mortals and of angels, but do not have love, I am a noisy gong or a clanging cymbal. And if I have prophetic powers, and understand all the mysteries and all knowledge... but do not have love, I am nothing.

I Corinthians 12:31 – 13:2

It is interesting that the handbook says something very similar when it points out the importance of recognising:

the extent to which pupils, parents and staff are committed to the vision and ambition of leaders, managers and governors. (p. 41)

This vision is not an individual or personal vision but one that emanates from Jesus Christ himself.

Modern Stained Glass, *The Call of the First Disciples*

Monitoring and evaluating school performance is carried out by the head teacher, senior leaders and managers at all levels. The role of the governors is to ensure that they are kept well informed on a regular basis of progress and any areas where there may be concerns. Early recognition and intervention are key to turning a potentially failing situation around.

Understanding formative and summative assessment can be difficult and some governors feel out of their depth, but this is where you have another helpful opportunity to ask the assessment coordinator to attend part of a governors' meeting to take you through how the school's assessment policy and processes assist and inform learning. Teachers will be only too happy to help and pleased that governors are keen to learn. Discovering at the end of the year that there has been a problem is too late and is indicative of a governing body that has taken its eye off the ball. It is your role to ask how all groups of pupils are progressing according to internal and external targets as well as in relation to other schools nationally. Remember, look at every area of the pupils' life and learning, not just the core subjects.

Making sure that parents and carers are also kept well informed is very important. Attending a parents' evening even if you are not a parent is a very useful way of learning about how well the school is keeping in touch with families and hearing their concerns as well as gratitude. Or a more informal method is to be at the school gate with the head teacher to chat with parents, especially if you are a primary school. This is less possible for secondary schools; however, a regular governors' surgery where parents can drop in for a chat also works well.

Spiritual, moral, social and cultural education (SMSC) across the curriculum

The context for all learning in a Catholic school flows from the beliefs and values of Christianity and the teachings of the Catholic Church. These beliefs and values must permeate all aspects of the life and learning within the school. Naturally as governors we must be able to see evidence of these beliefs and values being taught and lived. We have already looked at this area in detail in the section on SMSC in Chapter 5 above (pp. 79-80). However, you will notice in the Ofsted *School Inspection Handbook* this requirement is very prominent throughout. As governors we need to be very clear about what we consider to be SMSC education and ensure that the section 5 inspectors are also clear about how the school is delivering this important learning. The recent focus on "British values" by Ofsted needs to be clearly articulated within SMSC education.

Have a look at the description in Chapter 5, as the table will help you to articulate in straightforward language exactly what we mean within the Catholic context and can be easily shared with your inspector responsible for inspecting SMSC.

Hopefully, your head teacher will have appointed a member of staff with experience in curriculum design and leadership to be responsible for this area. As governors it is vital that you know who this is and ask him or her to demonstrate how it is delivered, monitored and evaluated.

Is our curriculum broad and balanced?

This is not easy for governors to keep up with. Your head teacher will keep you informed of the frequent changes. However, don't wait to be told when these may be about to occur; be proactive because one thing you can be sure of is that more changes are sure to occur!

The national curriculum is disapplied in 2014/15 in English, mathematics and science for Years 2, 6, 10 and 11; in 2015/16 in English, mathematics and science in Year 11, and in science in Year 10; and in 2016/17 in science in Year 11. (p. 42, n. 37)

Knowing that changes are coming also means knowing what they are and the impact on teachers and pupils. The need for retraining, new resources and communication with parents and carers is no small task. Our responsibility lies in familiarising ourselves, keeping abreast of the changes and supporting the head teacher and his or her team as they endeavour to introduce change, and then monitoring how it is working.

Staying focused on our core mission

I will never forget the moment when a well-known priest, addressing a full auditorium of head teachers on the mission of their schools, said:

What are we educating our children for? We are educating our children for their death.

You can imagine how that grabbed everyone's attention! How true it is. We are educating our children for that moment of encounter with their Creator God. Nothing less. How they come to that moment we have no control over. In the meantime it is essential that we do all we can to help them find that special gift that each one has been entrusted with so that in that moment of encounter with their God, which we call death, they will have completed all that they have been entrusted with. Job well done!

Section 5 will look closely at careers advice and support. Sadly, this has not always been to the forefront of some schools' agenda. It is essential that we help young people to discover their gifts and use them in modern Britain. It would be very helpful for governors to visit the careers department, and speak with pupils and staff about the advice, help and support that is on offer.

Keeping safe

There is no lack of training available for governors on the whole area of safeguarding. However, making sure that every governor is up to date sometimes gets overlooked. This area must be revisited annually and recorded; the inspectors will check. Make sure that you have an appointed governor for safeguarding. This governor can then work closely with the member of staff responsible for safeguarding to ensure that policies and procedures are up to date.

(For full details see "Inspecting safeguarding in maintained schools and academies", Ofsted, 2014: **www.ofsted.gov.uk/resources/140143**. Also the Ofsted *Governors' Handbook*, September 2014, section 4.9, "Safeguarding and promoting the welfare of pupils".)

Caring for those in the greatest need

A considerable amount of money has been given to

schools under the heading of pupil premium. The Catholic Church has always considered those in the greatest need in society to be our first priority:

People who are poor and vulnerable have a special place in Catholic teaching: this is what is meant by the "preferential option for the poor".

Catholic Bishops' Conference of England and Wales, *The Common Good and the Catholic Church's Social Teaching*, 1996

While few would argue with this statement by the bishops of England and Wales, putting it into practice is challenging. When we set our governance within the context of the mission of the Church our choices are clearly defined. Carrying them out is the challenge. However,

Scripture tells us we will be judged by our response to the "least of these", in which we see the suffering face of Christ himself. Humanity is one family despite differences of nationality or race. The poor are not a burden; they are our brothers and sisters.

The Common Good

Governors are accountable for their monitoring and evaluation of the use of these finances, which we must publish on the school website. We need to ask the head teacher to show how this money has made a difference to those children who really need it. However, your head teacher will explain that there are children who do not fit the government's criteria for this funding but are also in need. Once more our agenda is not limited by government criteria as we seek to find ways of meeting the needs of all our pupils. Often this means hard choices for governors. In terms of the section 5 inspection, being able to show how the governors are aware that they have a responsibility for responding to the particular needs of all children regardless of the pupil premium criteria shows very good practice.

The governors' role in holding the head teacher to account

Performance management is long established in schools. Setting of clear, measurable targets is a key factor for a successful outcome. However, it is not unusual for governors to agree targets with their head teacher that have no direct reference to the ongoing development of the school's core purpose. The place of the head teacher as the role model and primary leader of the school as a Catholic learning community must be part of the annual appraisal process. It is important to agree on one target that specifically focuses on ensuring the ongoing development of one of the following areas in just the same way that you would expect a professional regular review, evaluation and updating of any other area.

Some suggestions for possible areas for targets

- The theological and spiritual development of the head teacher
- The theological and spiritual development of middle leaders
- The theological and spiritual development of all staff

- Review of the mission statement to ensure that it is contemporary, child friendly and fit for purpose

- Developing leadership and competency across the school in leading and developing prayer and worship

- Continuing to promote the development of religious education and SMSC so that they are the lead academic areas throughout the school.

As governors we will be inspected on how well we have held our head teacher and all leaders across the school to account. It is also important to familiarise governors with the "Teachers' Standards". Your head teacher will be able to provide these for you. In this way you will have a very clear understanding of exactly what is expected by the government of teachers at all levels. This is very important because governors need to be able to demonstrate that they know and can point to evidence that the head teacher and leadership team are monitoring and evaluating standards of teaching and learning and are rigorously supporting all teachers in their efforts to raise standards to the highest possible level. Although academies do not have to apply the "Teachers' Standards" as part of their performance management arrangements, they do need to demonstrate how teachers are maintaining the highest possible professional standards. In the few cases where teachers are not performing well, inspectors will look at what the leadership of the school is doing to support and hold underperforming staff to account. This will need to be evidenced in the school's use of the performance management process throughout.

Setting, monitoring and evaluating the school's strategic direction

Producing a school development plan is a complex, professional task. Governors do rely very much on their head teacher to guide and advise on where the school needs to go. However, the development plan is the responsibility of the governors and in the best schools the professional development of the governing body, their key areas for action and regular skills audit are all incorporated into the development plan. Therefore it needs to be discussed, developed and agreed with all governors and the head teacher. As governors and senior leadership work together to formulate the whole school development plan, you will be able to ask those key questions about what needs to improve and how it is going to be done. Remember, governors are not about the "How" of development but are about the "What" and the "Why". The *School Inspection Handbook* makes this very clear when it states that inspectors are to consider whether governors:

provide challenge and hold the headteacher and other senior leaders to account for improving the quality of teaching, pupils' achievement and pupils' behaviour and safety, including by using the data dashboard, other progress data, examination outcomes and test results; or whether they hinder school improvement by failing to tackle key concerns or developing their own skills. (p. 48)

The best head teachers will always welcome your questions and requests for information. This professional dialogue helps everyone to clarify their thinking and set priorities. Inspectors very quickly pick up on the degree to which governors really know and have been part of this process or not.

Getting the right governors in place
This brief outline of what governors need to be aware of when faced with Ofsted can seem an unrealistic task for people who are not professional educators. Not everyone needs to be an expert in every area. What is necessary is that every member of the governing body is using his or her particular expertise to the full and that all governors are aware of who can supply the more detailed information on each particular area. All schools need to carry out regular skills audits to ensure they are fit for purpose.

Be prepared – on call – plan B
As we know there is a very short amount of time between the section 5 Ofsted phone call and the inspectors' arrival. So if you know that it is highly likely you will receive a visit in a particular term, then be ready and up to speed. Unfortunately many schools have found that they wait several terms after their due date. This is not easy for the leadership to manage. However, it is better to be ready than to leave it to chance. It is not uncommon for governors to suddenly discover that they can't get free from work in order to attend an interview with inspectors the next day, especially if they are travelling or out of the country. Therefore it is always wise to ensure the vice chair or a foundation governor or equivalent board member is fully prepared and up to speed, to step in if necessary.

What do we need to do for the section 48 inspection?

Every diocese has its own framework and procedures for carrying out section 48 inspections. It is important that as many governors as possible attend training on what is required of them during a diocesan section 48 inspection. Much energy goes into preparing for the Ofsted section 5 inspection. However, as important as the section 5 inspection is, the section 48 inspection is the critical part of the whole process. This is our core purpose – educating our children and young people in who they are, where they come from, why they are here and where they are going. As mentioned previously, the entire enterprise is about the transformation of society – building the kingdom of God. If we are not doing that, then the school must close.

How can governors prepare for the section 48 inspection?

Have a look at the diocesan framework for inspection – it will be on your diocesan website. Although each diocese has its own framework they all cover the same key areas.

Focus 1. Classroom religious education
The first aim of classroom religious education is to ensure that pupils are religiously literate in the teachings and traditions of the Catholic faith, which means that they can demonstrate that they know, understand and appreciate the importance of religious faith and practice in everyday life.

Inspectors will look at how well the *Religious Education Curriculum Directory for Catholic Schools and Colleges in England and Wales* (*RECD*) is being covered and taught.

They will assess the effectiveness of the leadership and management of religious education; the quality of teaching; pupil achievement, attainment and progress.

Inspectors will assess the quality, effectiveness of leadership and management of religious education throughout the school.

Focus 2. The Catholic life of the school
The inspectors will look closely at the commitment and effectiveness of the leadership and management, including governors, in promoting the Catholic life of the school. As we have mentioned earlier, from the mission statement, aims and objectives and strategic planning of the school, inspectors will be able to identify what the school holds as its core purpose and mission. Throughout the time the inspectors are in the school they will be evaluating how well pupils experience the integration of faith and life throughout all areas of school life.

Evidence for this will be seen through the place of religious education as the core of the core curriculum, informing all other areas. The bishops insist on it taking not less than 10% of the curriculum time (excluding prayer and worship). As governors we need to be clear about protecting RE from being watered down through moves to incorporate citizenship or PSHE into RE time in order to make space for other things! The *RECD* is very broad and spans a vast area of learning. Trying to cover it in 10% of curriculum time (5% for sixth forms) is a challenge. Encroaching on that time makes it impossible to deliver.

Appointing teachers of RE who are fit for purpose
Governors are the employers of all staff in the school. It is particularly important to make sure that those who are teaching RE are competent to do so. Finding teachers with the right RE qualifications is not easy. Sometimes it is necessary to retrain existing teachers from other departments or give extra support so that teachers are confident and competent in their delivery. As governors we need to keep a close eye on how much support and training RE staff are getting. If there are concerns, act sooner rather than later.

Prayer, worship and liturgy – for the whole school community

Inspectors will explore how prayer, worship and liturgy are being taught and experienced throughout the school. As governors we need to support all staff working with the pupils in understanding each of these areas and be confident that they are able to deliver. Furthermore, governors need to have a clear idea of how effective the prayer and worship life of the school is.

The commitment and contribution to the common good

Much has already been said about this earlier; however, governors need to be aware of the ways in which teaching for social justice is being delivered across the school as well as in RE lessons. SMSC education (including "British values") will also contribute to this area of learning. However, it is not just an academic endeavour. Governors need to know how commitment to the common good and education for justice, peace and the social teaching of the Church are actually being lived out and experienced by the pupils and adults in the school. Clear examples and evidence will help in discussions with the inspectors.

Home, school and parish

This is not an easy area, particularly as family life is constantly under pressure and parishes, although very important, see few families who have children at the school.

Home links are usually a strength of Catholic schools and generally parents feel well supported in times of difficulty. However, it is the large numbers of parents and carers who are quietly present that we need to be aware of. How do they feel about their children's learning? After all, the Church reminds us that "Parents are the first educators of their children" and schools are working in partnership with them, not for them. A thorough check of home links will prepare the governors well for questions concerning this area for both section 5 and section 48 inspections.

Schools can do, and in many cases are doing, a good deal to try to open doorways into parish life for their young people. As governors we will be concerned about this and have many initiatives in place. Before the inspection, revisit this area and try to identify the effectiveness of what is being done already and how you might build on it. Don't just leave it all to Father!

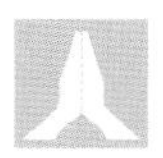

Reflection

It was said to a teacher, "I cannot hear what you say for listening to what you are." Truth and preaching are both "truth through personality".

William Barclay, *The Gospel of Luke*
(Edinburgh: Saint Andrew Press, 1953), p. 97

The integral formation of the human person, which is the purpose of education, includes the development of all the human faculties of the students, together with preparation for professional life, formation of ethical and social awareness, becoming aware of the transcendental, and religious education. Every school, and every educator in the school, ought to be striving "to form strong and responsible individuals, who are capable of making free and correct choices", thus preparing young people "to open themselves more and more to reality, and to form in themselves a clear idea of the meaning of life".

Sacred Congregation for Catholic Education,
Lay Catholics in Schools: Witnesses to Faith (1982),17

The greatest challenge to Catholic education... today, and the greatest contribution that authentically Catholic education can make... is to restore to that culture the conviction that human beings can grasp the truth of things, and in grasping that truth can know their duties to God, to themselves and their neighbours... The contemporary world urgently needs the service of educational institutions which uphold and teach that truth is, "that fundamental value without which freedom, justice, and human dignity are extinguished" (Veritatis Splendor, 4).

John Paul II, Address to the Bishops of the Ecclesiastical Regions of Chicago, Indianapolis and Milwaukee on their "Ad Limina" Visit, 30 May 1998

Modern man listens more willingly to witnesses than to teachers, and if he does listen to teachers, it is because they are witnesses.

Paul VI, *Evangelii Nuntiandi*,
"Evangelisation in the Modern World", 41

REFLECTION POINTS

- As you prepare for your inspection do you have the impression when you enter your school that you are entering a new environment, one illumined by the light of faith, with its own unique characteristics?
- How well do you feel you know your school and can you identify areas that you would like to see developed further?
- Who are the people that you feel you need to be more aware of and whose work you should celebrate?
- Can you identify one area of training you would like to undertake to improve as a governor?
- Do you and your governors celebrate their mission? If not, how might you do this?

CHAPTER 7

The role of the priest on the governing body

Education ought to teach how to be in love always and what to be in love with.

A.Clutton-Brock

It is important for the parish priest to be part of the governing body of a school in his parish. However, owing to the falling numbers of priests available to serve as governors, appointing priests to governing bodies is becoming increasingly difficult for the bishops. This is a serious situation as the priest has a particular role to play as a governor of the school, a role that is often both challenging for the priest and can lead him into difficult situations. In order to explore the unique contribution of the priest as a governor, it is helpful to listen to a variety of serving priests from varied backgrounds sharing their thoughts and hopes in their role as priest governor.

Canon Tony McBride – Episcopal Vicar for Education, Diocese of Salford, and foundation governor

Canon, how is the role of the priest any different from that of any other foundation governor?
The Catholic school is primarily part of the mission of evangelisation of the Church and so the bishop has prime responsibility for the education of Catholics in his diocese. The parish priest, in cooperation with assistant priests, parents and teachers, has responsibility for the Catholic education of children. Therefore you can see that immediately the priest has a very wide brief, which is enshrined in Canon Law. Canon 528 §1 stipulates the responsibilities of a parish priest in relation to Catholic education within his own parish in collaboration with the bishop and the Christian faithful:

He is to have a special care for the Catholic education of children and young people. With the collaboration of Christ's faithful, he is to make every effort to bring the gospel message to those also who have given up religious practice or who do not profess the true faith.

That particular part of Canon Law shows the relationship between the mission of the local parish and the mission of the school: to provide a Catholic education for the children and, through the work of education, call those who have ceased in the practice of their faith back to the full practice of their religion. That is why a Catholic school has a duty to accept all children who have been baptised in the Catholic Church and not just those whose parents go to Mass on Sunday.

I am glad to hear you say that the Catholic school is for every baptised Catholic, but I am not sure that all priests see it that way.
Yes, there are some practices that exclude children who come from non Mass-going families, but I am not happy about that because God, as a loving Father, is never content to leave his children in ignorance nor to allow them to live in error. The work of the parish priest and those who have the responsibility of educating our children in Catholic schools needs to be imbued with a spirit of cooperation and co-responsibility. The charism of being able to work together for the good of all must be alive in those responsible for the Catholic education of children.

The parish priest and assistant priest are automatically the chaplains to any Catholic school within the parish in which they have been appointed by the bishop to serve as priests. As such they are there to safeguard the teaching of the faith and to be a mentor and support to pupils and staff alike in the ways of faith. This is why in the Diocese of Salford we do not want parish priests to be Chairs of governors in their parish schools. Their responsibilities as priests go beyond the governance and management of our schools, although they are normally part of the governing body as foundation governors.

I have come across governing bodies who think that the priest must have the last word. They are very concerned about "not upsetting Father".
So have I! But that is a misunderstanding that should be quickly put right by the priest governor. He is not the "last word" on all matters, although theologically the priest may well be. Being a priest governor requires the parish priest to have that spirit of co-responsibility which respects the views of others and means he is never a dictator within his community. The parish priest should be the centre of unity in his parish, just as the bishop is in the diocese and the Pope is in the universal Church. He should never be a cause of division or conflict. The priest foundation governor has, in law, just one vote within the governing body, but his voice, like that of the good shepherd, should be heard and respected as the "Father" of the whole parish community, including the parish school.

Canon, you have had a lifetime's experience in Catholic education, but in this fast-changing arena do you feel equipped for the post of foundation governor?
On one level, a priest has the "potential" to be a foundation governor by his training as a leader in the

Catholic community. However, the virtue of humility should tell him that "he doesn't know it all". A school governor needs to know what the government requires of any school governor as well as what Canon Law states about a priest governor. He needs to treat his governorship as an invitation to serve on a "corporate body" and not in an "executive" way. Collaborative ministry is at the heart of this. The priest governor needs to give an example of leadership to other governors by going on the relevant courses and learning with them. What I find really difficult is trying to keep up with the constant changes coming from the government.

What further support do you feel the diocese should give?

Clearly stated guidelines for priest governors should be prepared and given, with the authority of the bishop, on each new appointment. Sometimes, because priests are not sure of what they should be doing, they use their "authority" as parish priest in an overbearing way; often with the best of intentions, but always inappropriately. The Church is not a democracy, but a governing body is part of the democracy in which we live. Persuasion rather than dictatorship should be the order of the day.

On a personal note, what do you enjoy about being a governor?

As a governor you have a practical say in the development of the faith in pupils, staff and parents. This should be a joyful opportunity for any priest who is a governor of a school. It is part of his basic reason for being in the leadership role he undertakes as parish priest. An understanding of the Catholic school as a primary arm of evangelisation is essential to this vision, but always in a collaborative way: I try to keep John 10:10 and Matthew 20:28 before me at all times as a governor.

What do you find challenging or difficult?

A person who is schooled in the ways of living required of a follower of Jesus Christ always finds it difficult to live with the demands of "Caesar" and the demands of the Gospel. The failure of so many to live up to the teachings of Christ and his Church can be a frustration, even given that a priest, too, is a sinner. It is more the fact that so many people do not even begin to appreciate the demands of the faith and what parents instigated by having their child baptised. I suppose it is the ignorance among so many that is most frustrating, and yet the whole purpose of the Catholic school is to do something about that ignorance. The temptation is always to work with the presupposition that "Father knows best" and that is when other real problems emerge. There are many good priests who can daily make the distinction between the "sinner" and the "sin" and so, like Pope Francis, welcome all comers. Above all, the virtues of patience and tolerance are needed here.

What advice would you give to your brother priests about being a governor?

Much of the above, but most of all not to go into school with an "agenda" of your own. Yes, Christ and his Church have an agenda as adequately described in the documents of the Church on Catholic education, but how this agenda is achieved, with the people we have in that situation, is something that takes more than dogmatic statement. It requires most of all the ability to be a "witness" to what is needed. The words of St Francis, "Preach the Gospel at all times;

use words if necessary," are most apposite here, along with a good dollop of humility. We have much to learn.

To what extent do you see the Catholic school assisting the Church in its evangelising mission?
The main reason why the Church is involved in education is evangelical in nature. It is about educating in that "right thinking", "right attitude" and "right conduct" that bring together love of God and love of neighbour. That's why we should never use the tools of the enemy: force, fear, dictatorship and punishment. A Catholic school is an evangelising community of its very nature and so is not separate from parish, diocese or universal Church. Educating for eternal life is the prime purpose of the Catholic school and so every subject and every exercise in education must have that vision. It is partly about knowing "facts", but it is how we use those "facts" to encourage action that is most important. The method of Cardinal Joseph Cardijn, "see, judge, act", is a very useful tool for this practical evangelisation.

Fr Shaun Middleton – Dean, North Harrow, Middlesex, and foundation governor

Father Shaun, how do you see your role as a priest on the governing body?
The image I would use is that of a bridge. Bridges at their best provide access and connect people. One of the most important of these connections is between the head teacher and the priest. The head teacher is often carrying many really difficult and confidential

issues. Heads need to know that there is someone safe that they can confide in and, above all, someone who will just listen to them. Naturally there are challenges. Schools are highly professional places and the teachers working in them really do know what they are doing. We priests need to recognise that and learn from them.

What do you find challenging?
A lot of things! One pet hate of mine is educational acronyms. It took me years to discover that an "SMSA" was what used to be called a "dinner lady"! Also there is just so much paperwork to read, which is littered with language that, unless you are a professional educationalist, can be excluding. I have adopted the role of "gentleman amateur"; I am the one who will usually say, "Sorry, I don't understand

that," or "Can you tell me what that means?" I think it's important not to be terrified by a language that I don't understand, so I always ask politely for someone to be kind enough to enlighten me as to what on earth we are talking about. You can usually see the look of relief on the other governors' faces when this happens.

What do you enjoy about your role?
I enjoy learning something new about education and children – that's great fun! However, I think it is important to go out of one's comfort zone in order to see things from another perspective. Priests can get stuck on the "Committee for the Catholic life of the school" or the "Curriculum RE committee". I always try to go for something I know very little about so that I can learn. A fresh pair of eyes is no bad thing.

What advice would you give to a newly ordained priest who has been appointed a governor?
Get some training, though there is not too much out there, and above all do your homework. People in school have gone to a great deal of trouble to prepare papers for the governors. Read them. Note the questions you want to ask and get involved. We need to remember that education is a shared endeavour. Watch your attitude and your language. It is important to resist the temptation to refer to the school as "my school". It is "our school". Vatican II asks us to encourage collaborative ministry between the clergy and the laity for the betterment of society and to grow in virtue. Where better to do this than in our local parish school?

How do you see yourself supporting the teaching of the faith in school?
My role is not to interfere, but to respond to what I see happening. I have to ensure that my response is measured and based on a desire to collaborate with the senior management team, with teachers and with the parents. A good example of this occurred last term. I was asked to hear confession for those young people being confirmed. Repeatedly, I heard, "Bless me, Father, this is my second confession." I was shocked! So in collaboration with the school we began a whole catechesis using the scripture character Nicodemus to illustrate our need to examine – confess – grow. This really challenged me. How, I asked myself, can I take what I can offer – the richness of our sacramental life – so that it really makes a difference in the lives of the children and therefore the school?

Father Shaun, you are an experienced governor. What advice would you give to the diocese in order to support the clergy working in schools?
We must support our priests more. There is far too much attention given to administration rather than mission. The role of the priest governor should be part of seminary training, and not just a one-off talk. It would also be good for newly ordained priests to meet with members of the diocesan education department so that experiences can be shared. The school is a major place of encounter between priest and people. Many priests do their best, but I think they would agree that they are ill prepared for the world of education today.

What would you say is the mission of the Catholic school in our country today?
To change the world. Nothing less than the transformation of society. We do this through outstanding education, which presents an alternative world view – Jesus Christ as the way, the truth and the life. Learning needs to be challenging but above all it needs to be fun!

Fr Thomas Wilberforce CSSp – Governor and chaplain working in St Peter's RC High School, Manchester

Father Thomas comes from Ghana, and has been working in schools for the past four years – three of them as school chaplain at St Peter's for four days a week.

Father Thomas, how do you find working as a priest in this country?
That is a good question! I still count myself as new to the country. I come from a very different culture and it takes time to understand and be able to be effective in such a completely new environment. In Ghana a priest is automatically respected by the people. Here that respect is not automatic – you have to earn it. That was hard for me at first; in fact, if I am truthful, it was a big shock! Now I prefer this way. It is more authentic.

How do you see your role as a governor?
Sometimes I find it difficult because I have a dual role. I am the chaplain for everyone in the school and I am also a foundation governor. It is not always easy to separate the two when I meet with staff. I have to be very clear which role I am in and make that clear to the person I am listening to. It is about having and operating within boundaries. Generally it works but I must be very careful in governors' meetings that I don't muddy the waters. Working with the children is not an issue. To them I am simply the chaplain and they know they can trust me and rely on me to be there for them in good times and when in difficulty.

What training and support did you have to be a governor?
Very little. I had to find out and be proactive. There wasn't much available in the diocese, but thankfully that is much better now. We can go on all of the CPDF (continuing professional development and formation) training days for teachers as well as attending specific governors' days. I go as much as possible, but it is not always easy on weekdays.

There are a good number of overseas priests coming to the country now and I think there need to be particular days for them. We have very different issues from people who have been born and grown up in this country. It is easy for us to give offence or be offended simply because we don't understand one another's culture.

How do you see your role as critical friend of the head teacher?
I was shocked when I first heard this! At home you would never criticise the head teacher. That would be very rude and disrespectful. However, I have come to understand how important this critical friend role is. It is important to hold all our discussion as a dialogue between two equals on the same mission, both respecting the other while not being afraid to challenge in order to better understand and move the school forward.

Is there an area of governorship that causes you the most concern?
Yes. It is the tension that arises quite often between the need to be as high as you can up the league tables and at the same time making sure that everything we do is permeated and driven by the Gospel and person of Jesus Christ. Our faith is the most important part of who we are. I also worry about how we as governors can help all our teachers to know more about Jesus Christ. I agree with Pope Francis when he says we are not just disciples, but missionary disciples. There is so much to be done and so few to do it.

Canon Paul McAleenan – Parish priest, Watford, and foundation governor

Father Paul, how do you feel about being a governor of a Catholic school?
Now that I have been a Catholic school governor for over twenty years, how I feel about the role of the priest hasn't changed, apart from the initial enthusiasm. I have never been a governor of a non-denominational school but sometimes I wonder whether 95% of the agenda would be similar if I was. Of course, I have to remind myself, it is that remaining 5% that differentiates the Catholic school and gives it its particular character. School governors' meetings do not excite me; the broad range of topics of the agendas, from the mundane to the specialist areas, creates a feeling of little to contribute, apart from one's own specialist area: Catholic life and the school's relationships with diocese and parish. A priest, of course, is a foundation governor, representing the trustees; as such he has duties and obligations that he must faithfully observe, such as preparing for attending governors' meetings.

Do you think priests are given enough training and support for this role?
Very good training is provided by local education authorities for all governors. I think that specific training for the priest as a governor is tied up with his priesthood training as in this role, as in all others, he is a representative of the bishop. It is up to the individual priest to build relationships with the staff of schools, students and their families. In my experience diocesan education authorities have been able to assist me with any difficulties or queries, particularly any legal ones I may have had.

As a governor, what hopes do you have for the future of Catholic education?
I remember reading somewhere: "Education is what is left after you've forgotten everything you've ever learned." What does one remember from school and schooling? Isn't it, above all, the formation one received that provides one's identity, one's place in the world? It is encouraging that so many Catholic schools have permanent visual images, crucifixes, statues and seasonal mosaics, which impress young, impressionable minds and visitors alike, reminding all about the school's foundational beliefs. I would hope that the doctrine behind these visible fixtures can be translated in classrooms, providing young people with language so that they can express who they are. It is very surprising sometimes to encounter those who have completed both primary and secondary Catholic education but are unaware of the basics of Catholic sacramental teaching, particularly on marriage.

What do you see to be the greatest challenges facing Catholic schools today?
I think it is understanding the difference between education and Catholic education. Is there a difference in the minds of many when applying for schools for their children? What does the prefix "Catholic" mean or add? Often the answer is "discipline", meaning "not unruly". The fact that many of our Catholic school attendees are non-practising has not lessened the Catholicity of our schools, all credit to heads and senior management. The greatest challenge is to maintain this Catholic identity at a time when some think it better to discard religious identity in schools. Furthermore, to fulfil the commandment to "love God and neighbour", delivery of the curriculum must form future adults aware of the social dimension of the Gospel.

Father Paul, if the cardinal were to ask you for one wish for Catholic education, what would it be?
If anyone were to ask me, I would be inclined to answer, "Is it necessary to filter Catholic school applications through the priest?" Apart from the fact that at times it seems like a full-time occupation from late September till April, does it effectively and positively discriminate in the way intended? It doesn't answer the question posed, of course, it leads to more questions. I think, particularly in the larger towns of Hertfordshire, the demand for more places will increase due to housing developments and the movement of population, including Catholics, northwards from London, and the settlement of Catholic migrants in this area. The question that I appreciate those concerned with Catholic education

in Westminster have always asked needs to continue: "Are there enough places in our schools for those who desire a Catholic education?"

Fr Christopher Gorton – Parish priest in Pendle, Lancashire, and school governor

Father Chris, how do you see your roles as both governor and parish priest working together to build up the links between school and parish?
As a parish priest and governor of three schools I have found it helpful using the image of garden and greenhouse – if the parish is the garden, then the schools are the greenhouses within it! For us this became a useful tool in planning and looking at how we can develop the relationship between the schools and the parish in a positive way for the future. This has now been presented to the head teachers of the diocese and at the next deanery conference will be presented to the clergy in the hope that this will help people value the correct relationship between school and parish and the unique role that schools have to play as chaplaincy provision for the young people in the parish.

So what you are doing is combining the school chaplaincy project with the parish?
Exactly. We call it "Growing Together in Christ – Schools as Chaplaincy Provision Within the Parish".

What led you to this point?
I was recently asked to be part of a working group within the Diocese of Salford to consider the relationship between head teachers and parish priests that soon developed into a consideration of the relationship between schools and parishes themselves. After a full and frank exchange between head teachers and priests it became apparent that unrealistic expectations, often lingering from a previous era, placed a lot of pressure on both priests and head teachers and the relationship between the two. The idea of a code of practice was superseded by the idea of a celebration of good practice, which then morphed into creating different models to enable discussion and dialogue in a positive manner.

How has the pupil chaplaincy initiative helped?
We have been thinking about how we can transfer the good practice within the school context into the parish and foster young leadership within the parish community. It was at this stage that I worked on the idea of school as chaplaincy within the parish. My background as a university chaplain gave me an

understanding of the role of a chaplaincy. To give just a brief working definition of where chaplaincy is usually provided: a group of people, in a particular situation, with a particular set of needs at a particular moment in their lives, with another group of people looking after them; for example, hospital, prison, military and university. Creating a chaplaincy enables a differentiated approach to preaching the kerygma: applying the incarnation, the life, teaching, death and resurrection of Christ, and the way people have responded to that in the Church, to the lives of people today. Schools have a particular group (children and young people), in a particular situation (school), with a particular set of needs (to be educated and discover their vocation), at a particular moment in their lives (growing up) and with another group of people looking after them (all who work in the school).

Some people are of the mind that the school is now the new parish. What is your response to this view?

School as chaplaincy within the parish emphasises the important, unique role that our schools have to play in relationship with and to the parish. Schools are not the new parishes. In my opinion this negates the specific role that schools have and, put bluntly, schools are not designed to meet the needs of all people who come into a geographical area, and they don't do baptisms, weddings and funerals! So I needed an image to emphasise the role of school as chaplaincy provision within the parish and chose the image of the parish as the garden and the schools as the greenhouses within it. The image allows people to explore the idea in their own way and as the bedrock for discussion that enables us to build in the right way for the future. It is a challenging image for all involved. It means that one cannot ignore the other. It challenges us to be "missionary disciples" and to look for ways forward together. But it is very necessary because there is always the danger that we could lose our schools or not want them if we are not clear on their specific role within the parish.

How do the rest of the governors feel about this idea?

Generally they are very happy about it because they can see growth and new life. What is essential is that everyone is fully informed and involved. Other schools and their parishes are keen to adopt this initiative and we are beginning to offer workshops to explore the way forward for other schools. To aid this idea we are now engaging in a poster campaign within the diocese (see video at **http://www.thegoodshepherdparish.co.uk/video-growing-together.php**) so that this image of garden and greenhouse and the identity of school as chaplaincy provision become part of the fabric of the decisions that we make within the schools and the parishes. Posters have been put in the staffroom, at the back of church, outside school; and postcards with the same image on notice boards and desks. The resources are also available online (**http://www.thegoodshepherdparish.co.uk/noticeboard.php?id=62&pt=news**) to use for Inset (in-service training), with governors, parents and parishioners. These include a fifteen-minute presentation introducing the idea, a ten-minute video of the photoshoot for the posters, the posters in different formats (PDF, PowerPoint and Publisher) allowing adaptation to local images and postcard and flyer information to help the discussion.

Ideas for developing the role of the priest in schools

Schools are delighted to discover that they have a priest who wants to visit and understands young people. Sadly, as our parish attendance at Mass continues to decline, many priests are at a loss to know how to deal with this situation. The reasons are many and often very complex. Doing nothing is not an option. Pope Francis is tirelessly encouraging everyone to be courageous, creative and innovative in finding new ways of reaching out to people.

Benedict XVI often spoke of a smaller, purer Church; Pope Francis is clear that what we must strive for is an inclusive Church, which is a

> *home for all… We have to find a new balance… otherwise even the moral edifice of the Church is likely to fall like a house of cards, losing the freshness and fragrance of the Gospel.*
>
> Interview with Fr Antonio Spadaro, August 2013

Many Catholic schools are equal in numbers to whole parishes and therefore offer critical opportunities for ministry and the building up of the community. Pope Francis is very clear in his call for the Church to go where the people are rather than remain behind structures and practices that no longer seem relevant to the majority of the laity who have simply walked away.

However, for some priests visiting any school is a daunting business. Either they are nervous because of all the media coverage regarding scandals or they are just not comfortable around small children or teenagers! Sadly, this is picked up very quickly by the school and can become a barrier. So what can one do?

Not everyone is comfortable in schools. For some priests a primary school can be very challenging simply because it is not always easy to know how to relate to small children. For others secondary schools seem overwhelming and often very fast moving and impersonal. Key to success is to simply be who you are, recognisable and known. Young people of all ages are usually very accepting as long as they know where they stand and whom they are dealing with. Long gone are the days when everyone in school knew who the priest was and he who they were. However, that does not need to be the case. The following ideas are from a wide range of schools who have worked very closely with their priest to try to build bridges into the parish and between the home and the school.

Opening the doors – building bridges between school, home and parish

The challenge facing many priests is how to engage with families who do not attend church. Catholic schools can be a very effective doorway into making contact with family members.

The following are a selection of ideas to help build bridges.

The school gate

While it can be very difficult to make contact with families of children who do not attend Mass on Sundays, there is a very important place of encounter at the school gate. You may be familiar with seeing the head teacher standing near the entrance to the school in the morning and the afternoon, as the children arrive and leave. This is because being present in this informal way is a valuable way of meeting and talking with parents and carers. The informal greeting, opportunity for a chat, all help to forge relationships and confidence. Many parents struggle with complex issues concerning their own lives, and their practice – or lack of it – of their faith, so they opt out altogether.

Instead of being just a church that welcomes and receives by keeping the doors open, let us try also to be a church that finds new roads, that is able to step outside itself and go to those who do not attend Mass, to those who have quit or are indifferent.

Pope Francis, Interview with Fr Antonio Spadaro, August 2013

It is important to be visible and reach out. It has long been my experience that when the priest is present in simple ways, offering friendship in a non-judgemental manner, meeting people where they are rather than where they are not, bridges begin to be built. For many the school gate, or in the case of larger schools the main entrance, is a far less threatening place of encounter and welcome. Never underestimate the power of a personal warm greeting, even if the response from some is little more than a nod or a grunt! In time relationships are forged and change comes. As a young teacher I learnt so much about the importance of personal recognition from an elderly Irish priest who cultivated an amazing ability to learn names and address eight hundred students personally each time he saw them. It became a source of entertainment to see if he could get a name straight. As a result he was rarely passed by. Knowing and remembering names is a gift I struggle with, but getting it right has a powerful impact.

Priest's/parish office in school

Parents who come to see the head teacher or senior staff come for a very wide range of reasons. Their child's education is the most common, but high on the list are also many pastoral concerns that call for family support or spiritual guidance and help. Issues include sorting out the many cases where pupils have not received the sacraments, family matters that could be well supported by the agencies within the parish, bereavements and sickness in families, and the many social issues that schools are continually being challenged to respond to, over and above their core purpose of education. Parents and carers who say that they have "lapsed" may find it too challenging to seek out help via the parish simply because of their own misconceptions of the response they will receive. However, if, as well as working with support agencies within the school, they are signposted to have a chat with the priest or pastoral assistant, by the school, in school, this can often be a very worthwhile opportunity to reopen a hitherto closed door.

I see clearly that the thing the Church needs most today is the ability to heal wounds and to warm the hearts of the faithful; it needs nearness, proximity.

Pope Francis, Interview with Fr Antonio Spadaro, August 2013

Invitation to the priest to come to an "at home" in the school

This idea has worked well in many schools where the form teacher/tutor prepares the class to put on a special tea or shared meal in the classroom to get to know their priest or priests. In a primary school the focus is usually on one priest; however, in a secondary school this can work just as well with the priest who is most associated with the school. The simple format of telling your story, what you enjoy doing, hobbies and interests, needs little preparation and provides a rare opportunity for pupils to have a chance to talk with a priest in a relaxed and familiar environment. Don't be surprised by the pupils' questions. Very quickly they will turn to questions such as, "Why did you become a priest?" and your views on many big questions of today. In return the pupils and staff will be delighted to receive an invitation from you to visit your home and see round the church, say a short prayer, light a candle for their families and see as much of the presbytery as appropriate while they enjoy tea with you!

Community builders – linking streets

This is a project that can easily be led by parishioners and the school, working together one year group at a time. The first step is to provide a large map of the school catchment area and divide it into areas/zones, indicating where the pupils come from. With a team of pupils, take one area at a time and invite the children to identify who lives in their neighbourhood. Cluster families together and ask the pupils to prepare invitations inviting neighbours to a social or prayer time or celebration for a special time of the year, to be held after school or if possible in the parish centre. The pupils are usually very good at getting one another to attend events if they have been part of the planning and are leading the event. Pupil leadership is key to the success of this project because they are far more effective in getting adults to attend functions that they are a part of. Keep the parish informed by inviting pupils to speak at Mass about their initiative. In this way neighbours begin to get to know each other as families and part of the parish community.

Charity work – workshops

Schools and parishes are well used to appeals for charity. However, this is only one way of responding to people in need. Christmas is a key example of a time when many people feel under pressure to spend money they don't have and for some what they would really like to do is make a difference to someone's life, but they feel they don't know how to go about it. Again this is where the school can be a focal point of meaningful interaction between families and the parish community.

Recycling of toys, bikes, scooters and second-hand unwanted gifts, as well as making Christmas cakes and puddings, are all excellent ways of involving as many people as possible in a worthwhile venture that helps many families. The parish priest, working with the school, advertises for adults who are willing to give time to repairing and refreshing items that can be reused as Christmas presents to be bought in a Christmas shop run by parishioners, parents and pupils in aid of a chosen charity. The shop can be located in the school or the parish, depending on which is the most suitable place for the maximum number of people to access. Keep the prices as reasonable as possible to ensure those in the greatest need can purchase items easily. Being present on the "shopping days" is another key moment of encounter with those who are rarely seen in the parish.

Adult classes, literacy, scripture, theology

The growing ethnic and cultural diversity of many parishes and pupils within our schools means that schools are often significantly stretched in providing the resources to respond to needs. The isolation that some families feel is compounded by a lack of language and literacy skills. Schools have very limited resources or time to respond to parental language and literacy needs. However, many are willing to make their premises available both during the day and after school for adult classes. This provides another opportunity for the parish to appeal for volunteers to help those new to the country in all sorts of ways, such as learning English, filling in forms, as well as befriending on many levels.

Adult formation in the faith is a great need. Although courses are run in the diocese, many of those who need it the most don't know that this is available or are not able to travel to the venue. Getting speakers can be difficult too. While the priest can and often does much to instruct and teach, it is also good to involve as many lay people as possible to lead or take part in sharing their faith stories. When this is set within the context of an event focusing on one of the following, accompanied by wine and cheese or similar refreshments, attendance tends to improve:

- How can we respond to the big issues concerning the Church today?

- An evening to discuss your questions about the Catholic Church

- How to answer the difficult questions your child may ask

- What does the Church really say about... (various topics)?

- What is the school teaching your children about Christianity and the Catholic Church?

Family-led liturgies in school

Class Masses are familiar and frequent in most schools. Usually the class prepares the liturgy with their tutor and the celebrant. An interesting variation on this practice is when families are invited to work with the school in preparing a Mass to be celebrated in the school and attended by the class and friends. This can be arranged on a rota, particularly if there is a special intention. Again it provides an opportunity for a more intimate experience where family members are involved and supported by the school. After Mass the family is invited to refreshments with the priest and an opportunity to talk together.

Using the liturgical life of the Church as a key focus

The liturgical calendar provides many creative opportunities for involvement between home, parish and school. Examples of these opportunities are found in many schools who are working with pupils and their families:

- Writing the bidding prayers at Mass and reading them.

- During Advent the pupils, supported by their teacher and with their families, compose an

Advent reflection, which is published in the newsletter and/or read out at Mass. If the family attends they can read their reflection out at an appropriate moment.

- During Lent divide up the Stations of the Cross and invite a family to adopt one station and to write a reflection and concluding prayer as part of the Stations of the Cross.

- At Pentecost invite as many families as possible to celebrate the birthday of the Church. Make the biggest possible bonfire to symbolise the Pentecost fire and organise a BBQ for all.

Men's night out

Most parish activities are predominantly run by women. The challenge facing many priests is how to reach out to the men whom they rarely have the chance to talk with or even see. In trying to find creative ways of getting men to take a higher profile, one parish I lived in hit upon the idea of organising activities entitled "Only men allowed". At first this seemed very exclusive; however, the parish priest had really hit on a very successful plan. Every two months he and a small group of men planned a day out to which all men and boys were invited! Activities ranged from hikes with frequent stops at various "watering holes", to day trips to France and other places of interest. Numbers quickly grew to the point that the women of the parish felt they were hard done by and the same had to be arranged for them! What was interesting was the way in which the men's days developed. The trip or journey became not only the means to a good day of fun and relaxation but the chance to talk and be together with their priest. What began with three people became over sixty in one year, because the days were fun as well as meeting a genuine need.

Therefore, carry out the ministry of Christ the Priest with constant joy and genuine love, attending not to your own concerns but to those of Jesus Christ. You are pastors, not functionaries. Be mediators, not intermediaries.

Pope Francis, Homily at Ordination Mass, April 2013

Men's retreat/women's retreat

It was from the "Only men allowed" days that the desire for spiritual nourishment grew. Again it was interesting that the men wanted their own days. What is important is going somewhere outside the parish so that no one is tempted to just pop home, come late or go early. It is important that people have the opportunity to stop and be quiet – a rare gift in today's world. Equally important is offering people the space to talk, be heard and prayed with as they try to cope with the day-to-day challenges of life.

I have a dogmatic certainty: God is in every person's life. God is in everyone's life. Even if the life of a person has been a disaster, even if it is destroyed by vices, drugs or anything else – God is in this person's life. You can, you must try to seek God in every human life. Although the life of a person is a land full of thorns and weeds, there is always a space in which the good seed can grow. You have to trust God.

Pope Francis, Interview with Father Antonio Spadaro, August 2013

Reflection

From St Ignatius of Antioch, writing to his friend Polycarp, Bishop of Smyrna. Ignatius was martyred by being thrown to the wild beasts in the Flavian amphitheatre in Rome in about AD 115.

You must do justice to your position
by showing the greatest diligence
Both in its temporal and spiritual duties.
Give thought especially to unity,
for there is nothing more important than this.
Make yourself the support of all and sundry,
as the Lord is to you,
and continue to bear lovingly with them all,
as you are doing at present.
Spend your time in constant prayer,
and beg for ever larger gifts of wisdom.
Be watchful and unsleeping in spirit.
Address yourself to people personally,
as is the way of God himself,
and carry the infirmities of them all
on your own shoulders,
as a good champion of Christ ought to do.
The heavier the labour, the richer the reward.

St Ignatius of Antioch, "Epistle to Polycarp", in *Early Christian Writers: The Apostolic Writings*, edited by A. Louth (London: Penguin Classics, 1968) p. 109

REFLECTION POINTS

- How do you feel about the views of the clergy in this chapter?
- Has anything challenged you in this chapter? Why?
- Are any "doorways" happening in your parish and how might these be further strengthened?
- What would you consider to be the similarities between the extract from St Ignatius and the mission of the Church today?
- What support do you feel you need to continue with your ministry in schools today?

CHAPTER 8

Prayers and praying together as governors

Do not forget to say your prayers. If your prayer is sincere, there will be every time you pray a new feeling containing an idea in it, an idea you did not know before, which will give fresh courage: you will then understand that prayer is education.

Fyodor Dostoevsky

Time to pray

When the agenda email drops into our inbox, how often do we all wilt at the sheer size and density of it! Every item is important and many need really careful consideration. All the more reason to take a few moments together to pause and allow God to guide our minds and hearts. What we are hoping for is that we will be able to pray with the heart of God, seeking to find the best in each one with no time for any form of injustice, prejudice or discrimination. Through prayer we seek to lose self and seek only the common good – to be people of great-heartedness, with a world heart reaching out to those in the greatest need. As Joan Chittister says:[1]

When, in prayer, we come to discover God's universal love we suddenly realise that God does not take sides, that we have no priority on God alone. We finally understand that the God we seek is the God of the world and so, to seek that God, we must develop hearts as big as the world ourselves.

As guardians of the vision we are called to become, says Chittister,

bigger than our single nation, broader than any one religion, truly Catholic – universal – in our cares and beliefs and commitments.

Where can I find prayers we can use?

Most dioceses have a governors' prayer, which is given to all governors to say at the start of their

[1] Quotes taken from Joan Chittister, *Essential Writings*, edited by M.L. Kownacki (Maryknoll, NY: Orbis Books, 2014)

meetings. This is helpful, but so often, if that is all, there is the danger that it becomes simply a "quick prayer"!

The following ideas and prayers are offered as a way of responding in prayer to the many and varied situations that governors find themselves in. This chapter is designed to be a resource to help develop the prayer life of your governing body and for individual governors.

To begin there are a wide range of online resources that you may find helpful.

Online resources

The following online sites are just a few of the many resources available today to help you to find out about the many different ways of praying as well as actually helping you to pray each day.

Some very helpful ideas: **www.prayforschools.org/resources/group-resources/inspirational-prayers/**

John Birch has written some really lovely prayers that you may well find helpful: **www.faithandworship.com/prayers**

A wide range of Christian prayers for all occasions: **www.churchyear.net/teacherprayers.html**

The Jesuits offer extensive resources, accompaniment and help for those wishing to develop their prayer life: **www.ignatianspirituality.com/ignatian-prayer/prayer-online/**

And: **jesuitprayer.org/**

A very good site for governor support in prayer from the Jesuits: **www.jesuitinstitute.org/**

The Franciscan friars have a helpful site: **www.franciscans.org.uk/franciscan-praying/prayers-of-saint-francis**

The Carmelites offer clear guidance on prayer and Lectio Divina for each day: **ocarm.org/en/content/ocarm/olmc/prayer-and-practices**

This site is very useful as it offers you a daily time of meditation that is simple yet challenging: **www.sacredspace.ie/**

Prayers for governors on different occasions

At the start of the year

God of love and mercy,
we praise you for the wonder of our being,
for all that you have created us to be.

Guide us, governors, staff and children as we begin a new school year.

Bless each one with your strength and grace as we grow in wisdom and knowledge, searching to understand the mystery and wonder of your creation.

We ask this through Jesus Christ our Lord.

Amen.

Governors' prayer for the New Year

All: Come, Holy Spirit! Come into our school at the start of the year.

Come Holy Spirit, enlighten our minds to your work

... in us;
... through us;
... for us.
May we all become the channel of your love for our community.

All: Come, Holy Spirit, help us to be people of courage

... to challenge
... to change
... to transform
So that we may be renewed in our commitment to build the kingdom of God.

All: Come, Holy Spirit! Come into our gathering at the start of this school year.

Come, Holy Spirit, and open our hearts to you speaking
... in our fellow governors;
... through our children;
... in our teachers and staff.
Inspire us to be a people of hope.

All: Come, Holy Spirit! Enlighten the eyes of our minds

... to see you in people who challenge us;
... to your working in situations we don't understand;
... to your moving gently in our hearts.
Help us to be a people of wisdom.

Amen.

Prayer for a willingness to serve others

Lord, make us instruments of your peace.
Where there is hatred, let us sow love;
where there is injury, pardon;
where there is discord, union;
where there is doubt, faith;
where there is despair, hope;
where there is darkness, light;
where there is sadness, joy.
Grant that we may not so much seek
to be consoled as to console;
to be understood as to understand;
to be loved as to love.
For it is in giving that we receive;
it is in pardoning that we are pardoned;
and it is in dying that we are born to eternal life.

Amen.

St Francis of Assisi

A prayer for positivity

Holy Spirit
Banish our spirit of criticism;
Replace it with a spirit of affirmation.
Help us to see the glass that is half full;
The essay that is half written;
The answer that is halfway correct.
Help us to see the many students with their hands up...
Not just the few who are shouting out!

Banish our spirit of self-resignation;
Replace it with a spirit of determination.
Help us to be bold and tenacious;
To believe in ourselves;

To believe in our colleagues;
To believe in our God;
To believe that all things are possible.
Banish our spirit of procrastination;
Replace it with a spirit of energy and action.
Help us to get ourselves organised,
So we can do the things we said we would do.
Give us a sense of purpose and direction;
Help us to praise students and co-workers who keep going...
Even when the going gets tough!

Amen.[2]

Prayers for our teachers and support staff

The best teacher (revised for the twenty-first century)

He never taught a lesson in a classroom.
He never used an interactive white board.
Not once did He use PowerPoint to make His case.
He did not have internet access... or a computer... or even electricity.

He was not trained by a university education department.
He never gained qualified teacher status.
He was never inspected by Ofsted.
He never crossed the teacher pay threshold.
He never spent time photocopying and laminating resources,
or putting up classroom displays.
He never handed out gold stars,
house points or certificates.
He never wrote end of year reports.
He never referred to the National Curriculum
or followed QCA guidelines.
He kept no records, gave no grades,
and His only text was ancient and well-worn.

His lessons were socially inclusive.
He taught the economically deprived as well as the wealthy;
He taught the physically disabled and the mentally ill
as well as those healthy in body and mind.

His teaching method was the same with all who came to hear and learn.
He opened eyes with faith,
He opened ears with simple truth,
and He opened hearts with love... a love born of forgiveness.

He challenged, inspired and healed those He taught.
He changed individuals and transformed communities.
Even so, He was never nominated for a Teacher of the Year Award
or knighted for His services to education.

And yet this quiet teacher from the hills of Galilee continues to feed the needs,
fulfil the hopes, and change the lives of many millions around the world,
for what He teaches brings heaven to earth
and reveals God's heart to all peoples everywhere.

Rupert Kaye

2 www.prayforschools.org/resources/group-resources/inspirational-prayers/

A prayer of thanks for all God's children

Lord our God
We thank you that you made each one of us in your image and likeness,
and that we are all your beloved children.

We pray for the children/students we teach.

We pray for children/students who... make us smile;
... challenge our way of thinking;
... test our patience;
... we find easy to like;
... we find difficult to like;
... are bright;
... are hardworking;
... find learning tough;
... get on our nerves;
... are a delight;
... like to laugh;
... always look sad;
... always look lost;
... talk all the time;
... never say a word;
... are easily overlooked;
... are impossible to ignore;
... remind us of ourselves when we were younger!

We thank you for all the children/students who have an impact on our lives
and for the privilege of having an impact on their lives.

Lord, help us not to label those we teach or to fall into the trap of thinking we have got them sussed. Help us to be open to new revelations and the work of your Holy Spirit in each of their lives.

Lord, use those we teach to teach us. Help us to be Christ-like at all times; seeing each one with your eyes and valuing them with your heart of love.
We ask this prayer in the name of Jesus the teacher.

Amen.

Rupert Kaye

A prayer before appointing a new head teacher

Father, you have entrusted us with the care of your children here in... (name of school). Help and guide our minds and hearts today to recognise the person you know we need to lead our school on the next part of its journey.
A journey in loving
A journey in learning
A journey in understanding
A journey in becoming
A journey in discovery
A journey in hope.

Open our hearts to hear and our minds to recognise your voice today.

Amen.

A prayer before appointing a new member of staff

Guide us, Lord Jesus, as we greet each candidate today.
May they feel secure and valued.
Inspire each one to be able to share with us their hopes and dreams for the children.
Together help us to discover if this is to be where they should be.
Enlighten our minds with your Holy Spirit so that

we may discover their gifts and talents.
May each one feel that they have given of their best.

Amen.

A prayer before the inspector calls

Lord Jesus, fill each one here in our school with your spirit of wisdom and understanding.

... Guide us in our answering
... Direct our questioning
... Lighten our worrying
... Strengthen our courage
... Enrich our teaching
... Steady our nerves
... Ignite our passion
... Gentle our speech
... Hold us in the palm of your hand.

And above all let us never forget that this is your work that we do. Be with us today so that we may be ever more true to our calling as teachers of your children, our brothers and sisters.

Amen.

A prayer for our children before SATs

Father of all our children, enlighten and encourage each child here today as they do their tests. We bless you for each one and thank you for the gift that they are for us. May they be able to recall all that you have helped us to teach them and feel proud of their achievements.

Amen.

A prayer before our pupils sit their final examinations

O God, help our students as they sit their examinations
to recall the things which they have learned and studied.
May they remember clearly and set down that which they know so well.
Steady their nerves and calm their minds,
doing justice for all their hard work.
May each one feel that they have achieved the very best they can be.

Amen.

A prayer for the end of term

Christ, our Teacher,
bless everyone in our school
as we come to the end of the year.
Pour out your loving grace
on all who have given so much,
asking only that each one may receive
that which you have prepared for them.
We give thanks for everyone in the school
for this year of nurturing and growth,
of laughter, of fun, of joy of discovery.
We give thanks for the challenges and achievements,
for the hard times, the misunderstandings and the joy of forgiveness.
Stay with us in our rest days
so that we may be renewed and restored.
Keep each one safe in your loving embrace
so that we may return renewed to continue
the ongoing discovery of your love.

Amen.

Prayer in times of trouble

I asked for strength that I might achieve;
I was made weak that I might learn humbly to obey.
I asked for health that I might do greater things;
I was given infirmity that I might do better things.
I asked for riches that I might be happy;
I was given poverty that I might be wise.
I asked for power that I might have the praise of men;
I was given weakness that I might feel the need of God.
I asked for all things that I might enjoy life;
I was given life that I might enjoy all things.
I got nothing that I had asked for,
but everything that I had hoped for.
Almost despite myself my unspoken prayers were answered;
I am, among all men, most richly blessed.

Unknown Confederate soldier

In times of rejoicing

Psalm 95

A Song of Praise and Joy

Come, let us praise the Lord!
Let us sing for joy to God, who protects us!
Let us come before him with thanksgiving
and sing joyful songs of praise.
For the Lord is a mighty God,
a mighty king over all the gods.
He rules over the whole earth,
from the deepest caves to the highest hills.
He rules over the sea, which he made;
the land also, which he himself formed.
Come, let us bow down and worship him;
let us kneel before the Lord, our Maker!
He is our God; we are the people he cares for,
the flock for which he provides.

Good News Bible

Advent

God of hope, who brought love into this world,
be the love that dwells between us.
God of hope, who brought peace into this world,
be the peace that dwells between us.
God of hope, who brought joy into this world,
be the joy that dwells between us.
God of hope, the rock we stand upon,
be the centre, the focus of our lives
always, and particularly this Advent time.[3]

Christmas

O sweet Child of Bethlehem,
grant that we may share with all our hearts
in this profound mystery of Christmas.
Put into the hearts of men and women this peace
for which they sometimes seek so desperately
and which you alone can give to them.
Help them to know one another better,
and to live as brothers and sisters,
children of the same Father.
Reveal to them also your beauty, holiness and purity.
Awaken in their hearts
love and gratitude for your infinite goodness.
Join them all together in your love.
And give us your heavenly peace.
Amen.

St John XXIII

[3] www.faithandworship.com/prayers_Advent.htm

Mary

"You will be with child and give birth to a son, and you are to give him the name Jesus. He will be great and will be called the Son of the Most High. The Lord God will give him the throne of his father David, and he will reign over the house of Jacob forever; his kingdom will never end."

Luke 1:31-33

When does an ordinary life
Become extraordinary
A mundane day
Become revolutionary
A moment in time
Change history?
When God enters in
Forgives sin
Allows us to
Begin again
When we repeat
Those words of Mary
"May it be to me
As you say"

"The Holy Spirit will come upon you, and the power of the Most High will overshadow you. So the holy one to be born will be called the Son of God. Even Elizabeth your relative is going to have a child in her old age, and she who was said to be barren is in her sixth month. For nothing is impossible with God."

All: "I am the Lord's servant," Mary answered. "May it be to me as you have said."

Luke 1:35-38

Lord God, you choose the very least
And raise us up to greatness
All: For nothing is impossible with God.
You take the weak, the poor and blind
And raise us out of darkness
All: For nothing is impossible with God.
Give thanks to the Lord, for he is good.
All: His love endures forever.
Give thanks to the God of gods.
All: His love endures forever.
Give thanks to the Lord of lords.
All: His love endures forever.

Teach us obedience, Lord
In every part of our lives
Ears to hear your word
Hands to do your work
Feet to walk your path
A heart for all your people
A mouth to shout your praise
A childlike faith
Humility
Confidence
That says
To the possible
And the impossible

All: I am the Lord's servant
May it be to me as you have said.

Amen.

John Birch

Candlemas

We praise you, our light and salvation
You are the joy of our life

We praise you, our light and salvation
May your light illumine our minds

We praise you, our light and salvation
Lighten our path as we seek to follow you

We praise you our light and salvation
Strengthen us as we journey to find you

We praise you, our light and salvation.

Lent

Grant me, O Lord my God, a mind to know you,
A heart to seek you,
Wisdom to find you,
Conduct pleasing to you,
Faithful perseverance in waiting for you,
And a hope of finally embracing you.

St Thomas Aquinas

Easter

Christ, Lord of life, raised up by the Father; we give you praise, honour and thanks
as we say:

All: Christ, you are our life.

Lord Jesus, light which has defeated darkness, lead your people into life, renew us with the gift of holiness – we gather in praise of your glory.

All: Christ, you are our life.

Lord, you walked the way of suffering and crucifixion – may we never lose heart as we each carry our own cross, remembering that it is you who walk with us.

All: Christ, you are our life.

Jesus, Son of the Father, our master and our brother, you have redeemed us and shown us the way to eternal happiness – may we never cease to follow you.

All: Christ, you are our life.

King of glory, we rejoice in the hope that we will see you coming in splendour
– may we see you face to face, and be transformed in your likeness.

All: Christ, you are our life.

Amen.

Pentecost

Lord Jesus, as God's Spirit came down and rested upon you,
may the same Spirit rest on us,
bestowing his sevenfold gifts.
First, grant us the gift of understanding,
by which your precepts may enlighten our minds.
Second, grant us counsel, by which we may follow
in your footsteps on the path of righteousness.
Third, grant us courage,
by which we may ward off the enemy's attacks.

Fourth, grant us knowledge,
by which we can distinguish good from evil.
Fifth, grant us piety,
by which we may acquire compassionate hearts.
Sixth, grant us fear,
by which we may draw back from evil
and submit to what is good.
Seventh, grant us wisdom,
that we may taste fully the life-giving sweetness of
your love.

Prayer of St Bonaventure to the Holy Spirit

Praying with scripture

To prepare for the prayer time arrange a simple focal point for everyone to focus on. A combination of some of the following:

- Cloth
- Bible
- Candle
- Picture or icon
- Flowers
- Artefact that is appropriate for the time of year.

It can sometimes help to create the right atmosphere to have some quiet music to accompany the prayer time, either throughout or at the beginning or end. If you are going to have it throughout, then use instrumental music that does not intrude into the prayer time.

At the start of the time of prayer invite everyone to read through the scripture extracts and select just one that seems to be speaking to them today. Stay with that verse or saying. After a few minutes invite each one simply to read out their verse. (Don't worry if more than one person has the same one.) Do this without commenting and allow God to speak to each one through the words of scripture.
After the last person has spoken leave a few moments' silence.

Invite people to spontaneously share their thoughts and prayers.

Use a simple response such as:

Lord, in your mercy;
hear our prayer.
or
Lord, hear us;
Lord, graciously hear us.

Examples of suitable scripture passages

I pray that you may have the power to comprehend, with all the saints, what is the breadth and length and height and depth, and to know the love of Christ that surpasses knowledge, so that you may be filled with all the fullness of God. **Ephesians 3:18-19**

Because you are children, God has sent the Spirit of his Son into our hearts, crying, "Abba! Father!"
So you are no longer a slave but a child, and if a child then also an heir, through God. **Galatians 4:6-7**

Ask, and it will be given to you; search, and you will find; knock, and the door will be opened for you. For everyone who asks receives, and everyone who searches finds, and for everyone who knocks, the door will be opened. **Matthew 7:7-8**

Love is patient; love is kind; love is not envious or boastful or arrogant or rude.
It does not insist on its own way; it is not irritable or resentful; it does not rejoice in wrongdoing, but rejoices in the truth. It bears all things, believes all things, hopes all things, endures all things.
1 Corinthians 13:4-7

So we do not lose heart. Even though our outer nature is wasting away, our inner nature is being renewed day by day. For this slight momentary affliction is preparing us for an eternal weight of glory beyond all measure, because we look not at what can be seen but at what cannot be seen; for what can be seen is temporary, but what cannot be seen is eternal. **2 Corinthians 4:16-18**

For God so loved the world that he gave his only Son, so that everyone who believes in him may not perish but may have eternal life. **John 3:16**

Jesus said to her, "Everyone who drinks of this water will be thirsty again, but those who drink of the water that I will give them will never be thirsty. The water that I will give will become in them a spring of water gushing up to eternal life." **John 4:13-14**

I came that they may have life, and have it abundantly. **John 10:10**

Jesus said to him, "I am the way, and the truth, and the life. No one comes to the Father except through me." **John 14:6**

But strive first for the kingdom of God and his righteousness, and all these things will be given to you as well. **Matthew 6:33**

In the same way, let your light shine before others, so that they may see your good works and give glory to your Father in heaven. **Matthew 5:16**

In everything do to others as you would have them do to you; for this is the law and the prophets.
Matthew 7:12

"You shall love the Lord your God with all your heart, and with all your soul, and with all your mind." This is the greatest and first commandment. And a second is like it: "You shall love your neighbour as yourself." On these two commandments hang all the law and the prophets. **Matthew 22:37-40**

For the Son of Man came not to be served but to serve, and to give his life a ransom for many.
Mark 10:45

Jesus answered him, "It is written, 'One does not live by bread alone.'" **Luke 4:4**

When he had finished speaking, he said to Simon, "Put out into the deep water and let down your nets for a catch." **Luke 5:4**

My mother and my brothers are those who hear the word of God and do it. **Luke 8:21**

Organising a retreat day for governors

Preparation

Finding a date

What is important is to give enough prior warning so that as many people as possible can come. You may also wish to join up with other Catholic schools in your area. Try to make it a day event: 10.00 am to 3.00 pm usually works well.

Choosing the venue

If possible don't have it in school unless you have beautiful surrounds. This is simply because governors who are teachers may well find it too distracting and feel the temptation to just pop off and "do an urgent task"! If they can't see it, it will wait. Try to choose somewhere reasonably local and with good facilities; if possible, a venue that provides a sit-down meal and refreshments.

Getting the theme right

It really helps to have a theme for the day that includes everyone and touches the core purpose of why you are governors and where you hope to go. Taking part in a retreat day offers the opportunity of making time to listen to what God may be trying to say to you in your personal and family life as well as in your ministry as a governor.

Finding a retreat leader

Not a governor of the schools attending the day! If you can't think of a suitable person, then contact the diocese and explain what you are hoping for and they should be able to provide you with suitable names.

Possible timetable

Refreshments on arrival and a warm welcome are always very important to help people settle.
This can then be followed by an opening prayer – something gentle and reflective.
Your morning should be broken up into a talk from the retreat leader followed by free quiet time for people to reflect, pray and, if possible, go for a walk. Time to be alone and think is rare for most governors who are extremely busy. So this is a rare moment.
Lunch should not be rushed. About an hour is good.
The afternoon can then be made up of another talk, time for reflection and free time.
The last hour can take several forms:

- Adoration
- Mass
- A guided meditation
- A para-liturgical celebration which someone leads.

Tea and farewells.

Reflection

Prayer takes place in the heart, not in the head.

Carlo Carretto, *The Desert in the City* (Fount, 1981)

Love to pray – feel the need to pray often through the day and take the trouble to pray. If you want to pray better, you must pray more. Prayer enlarges the heart until it is capable of containing God's gift of himself. Ask and seek and your heart will grow big enough to receive him and keep him as your own.

Quoted in *In the Silence of the Heart: Meditations by Mother Teresa*, edited by Kathryn Spink (Isis, 1985)

God will always answer our prayers; but He will answer them in His way, and His way will be the way of perfect wisdom and of perfect love. Often if He answered our prayers as we at that moment desire, it would be the worst thing possible for us, for in our ignorance we often ask for gifts which would be our ruin.

William Barclay, *The Gospel of Matthew* (Westminster, 1956)

REFLECTION POINTS

- Which of the reflection quotes do you feel expresses how you feel about prayer and why?
- What place does prayer play in your ministry as a governor?
- As a governing body, how comfortable are you giving time to prayer together?
- Are there resources that might help governors in their prayer?
- As governors, how do you think you could assist the school community in their understanding and growth in prayer?

Pope Francis' five-fingered prayer

Using the fingers on your hand, start with the thumb and pray these intentions in this order:

1. The thumb is the closest finger to you. So start praying for those who are closest to you. They are the persons easiest to remember. To pray for our dear ones is a "Sweet Obligation".

2. The next finger is the index. Pray for those who teach you, instruct you and heal you. They need the support and wisdom to show direction to others. Always keep them in your prayers.

3. The following finger is the tallest. It reminds us of our leaders, the governors and those who have authority. They need God's guidance.

4. The fourth finger is the ring finger. Even though it may surprise you, it is our weakest finger. It should remind us to pray for the weakest, the sick or those plagued by problems. They need your prayers.

5. And finally we have our smallest finger, the smallest of all. Your pinkie should remind you to pray for yourself. When you are done praying for the other four groups, you will be able to see your own needs but in the proper perspective, and also you will be able to pray for your own needs in a better way.